D1065377

DIAGNOSIS AND TREATMENT SELECTION FOR ANXIETY DISORDERS

Samuel Knapp, EdD
Halifax, Pennsylvania

Leon VandeCreek, PhD
Department of Psychology
Indiana University of Pennsylvania

Professional Resource Exchange, Inc.
Sarasota, Florida

Printed in the United States of America

Paperbound Edition ISBN: 0-943158-30-3
Library of Congress Catalog Number: 88-43469

The copy editor for this book was Barbara Robarge, the
production supervisor was Debbie Fink, the graphics
coordinator was Judy Warinner, and the cover designer
was Bill Tabler.

The views expressed here do not necessarily represent
those of the Pennsylvania Psychological Association.

PRACTITIONER'S
RESOURCE SERIES

Diagnosis and Treatment Selection for Anxiety Disorders

Peter A. Keller, PhD
Chair, Department of Psychology
Mansfield University
Mansfield, Pennsylvania

Antonio E. Puente, PhD
Associate Professor of Psychology
University of North Carolina at Wilmington
Wilmington, North Carolina

R. John Wakeman, PhD
Head, Department of Clinical Psychology
Ochsner Clinic and Ochsner Foundation Hospital
New Orleans, Louisiana

SERIES PREFACE

As a publisher of books, cassettes, and continuing education programs, the Professional Resource Exchange strives to provide mental health professionals with highly applied resources that can be used to enhance clinical skills and expand practical knowledge.

All of the titles in the *Practitioner's Resource Series* are designed to provide important new information on topics of vital concern to psychologists, clinical social workers, marriage and family therapists, psychiatrists, and other mental health professionals.

Although the focus and content of each book in this series will be quite different, there will be notable similarities:

1. Each title in the series will address a timely topic of critical clinical importance.
2. The target audience for each title will be practicing mental health professionals. Our authors were chosen for their ability to provide concrete "how-to-do-it" guidance to colleagues who are trying to increase their competence in dealing with complex clinical problems.
3. The information provided in these books will represent "state-of-the-art" information and techniques derived from both clinical experience and empirical research. Each of these guide books will include references and resources for those who wish to pursue more advanced study of the discussed topic.

4. The authors will provide numerous case studies, specific recommendations for practice, and the types of "nitty-gritty" details that clinicians need before they can incorporate new concepts and procedures into their practices.

We feel that one of the unique assets of the Professional Resource Exchange is that all of its editorial decisions are made by mental health professionals. The publisher, Larry Ritt, is a clinical psychologist and marriage and family therapist who maintains an active independent practice. The senior editor, Peter Keller, is a clinical psychologist who currently serves as chair of a psychology department and is actively involved in clinical training.

The editor of this series, Hal Smith, is a clinical psychologist in independent practice. He holds a diplomate in clinical psychology from the American Board of Professional Psychology, a diplomate in forensic psychology from the American Board of Forensic Psychology, and a diplomate in clinical neuropsychology from the American Board of Professional Neuropsychology. His specialties include clinical and forensic psychology, neuropsychology, stress management, management of chronic pain and psychophysiologic disorders, learning disabilities, interventions for spouse abusers, psychotherapy, psychodiagnostic evaluations, clinical hypnosis, and consultation.

We are also fortunate to have the services of an exceptionally well-qualified panel of consulting editors who assist in the selection and preparation of titles for this series: William D. Anton, Judith V. Becker, Philip C. Boswell, Florence Kaslow, Antonio E. Puente, and R. John Wakeman. Our consulting editors are all highly experienced clinicians. In addition, they have all made significant contributions to their professions as scholars, teachers, workshop leaders, researchers, and/or as authors and editors.

Lawrence G. Ritt, Publisher
Harold H. Smith, Jr., Series Editor

ABSTRACT

This guide presents current information on diagnosis and treatment selection for anxiety disorders. Each anxiety disorder listed in *DSM-III-R* is described and the latest research on differential diagnosis and frequent diagnostic complications and co-existing disorders is considered. Explicit decision rules are provided for treatment selection based on empirical research and clinical judgment. Specific psychological tests are recommended to supplement treatment interviews. Sample case vignettes are provided to illustrate the more common anxiety disorders. Although details on how to implement specific techniques are not provided, training materials are referenced for readers who want more information about treatment strategies.

TABLE OF CONTENTS

DIAGNOSIS AND TREATMENT SELECTION FOR ANXIETY DISORDERS

INTRODUCTION

The diagnosis and treatment of anxiety disorders have changed extensively in the past 15 years and especially in the last few years. Most of these changes have occurred because of the demonstrated effectiveness of behavioral and pharmacological treatments. Treatments that were experimental or novel 15 years ago are now part of standard treatment regimens. These treatments include the use of graduated exposure with panic disorders, response prevention with obsessive-compulsive disorders, and the use of "antidepressants" and alprazolam (Xanax) to suppress panic attacks. Some older treatments now are being applied with more success with other anxiety disorders. For example, psychoanalytic procedures, which had a poor track record with anxiety disorders, are being modified on the basis of recent information.

The third edition of the *Diagnostic and Statistical Manual of Mental Disorders (DSM-III)* (American Psychiatric Association, 1980) provided more precise descriptions and criteria for diagnoses of anxiety disorders than previous editions. The *DSM-III* eliminated the overly broad diagnosis of "anxiety state" and created the more specific diagnoses of *generalized anxiety disorder, agoraphobia with panic disorder, agoraphobia without panic disorder, panic disorder, social phobia, simple phobia, and post-traumatic stress disorder.* The *DSM-III* also provided reliable operational criteria to distinguish these diagnostic categories. This standardization allowed researchers to compare studies across a wide range of treatment settings and procedures.

The recent revision of the *DSM-III,* the *DSM-III-R* (American Psychiatric Association, 1987), used empirical research to further refine psychiatric diagnoses. Table 1 (p. 2) outlines the major differences between the *DSM-III* and the *DSM-III-R* for anxiety disorders.

In addition, the *DSM-III-R* has abolished most hierarchical rules. The hierarchical rules of the *DSM-III* required the clinician to follow a pre-determined sequence in making a diagnosis. For example, if a patient presented symptoms of depression and panic disorder under the *DSM-III,* then the diagnosis would be depression because the hierarchical rules required that the depression diagnosis take precedence over the panic disorder. However, anxiety disorders have high co-morbidity with each other and with other nonanxiety disorders, and

1

TABLE 1: COMPARISON OF <u>DSM-III</u> AND <u>DSM-III-R</u> CATEGORIES OF ANXIETY DISORDERS

<u>DSM-III</u>	<u>DSM-III-R</u>	<u>COMMENTS</u>
Agoraphobia with panic attacks.	Panic disorder with agoraphobia.	<u>DSM-III-R</u> places primary emphasis on the panic component.
Panic disorder.	Panic disorder without agoraphobia.	
Agoraphobia without panic attacks.	Agoraphobia without history of panic disorder.	Agoraphobia without panic attacks is quite rare.
Social phobia.	Social phobia.	
Simple phobia.	Simple phobia.	Includes blood, injury, and illness phobias.
Obsessive-compulsive disorder.	Obsessive-compulsive disorder.	
Generalized anxiety disorder.	Generalized anxiety disorder.	<u>DSM-III-R</u> lengthened the duration of generalized anxiety disorder from 1 to 6 months and expanded the symptom list.
Post-traumatic stress disorder.	Post-traumatic stress disorder.	More explicit definitions of severe stressors, and addition of symptoms commonly found in children.
Atypical anxiety disorder.	Anxiety disorder not otherwise specified.	

under the *DSM-III-R* rules these additional diagnoses may now be recognized.

The *DSM-III* and especially the *DSM-III-R* helped clarify the diagnosis of personality disorders which often co-exist with anxiety disorders. The identification of a co-existing personality disorder greatly aids in the total treatment of the anxiety patient.

The changes included in the *DSM-III-R* are consistent with current research on the differentiation of anxiety disorders. Table 2 (pp. 4-5) summarizes several demographic and clinical variables that characterize the different anxiety disorders.

THE INITIAL ASSESSMENT

The initial interviewing process should follow a funneling procedure in which the psychotherapist initially develops a broad picture of the patient's problems and gradually narrows them to more specific problems. In this initial phase, the psychotherapist should learn the patient's perceptions of problem areas and specific assets of each patient.

A comprehensive assessment should meet three major objectives: describe the presenting problem, aid in the selection of optimal treatment, and provide a means for evaluating treatment outcome. The traditional diagnostic label largely fulfills the first goal of describing the patient's problem. A diagnosis, however, is often not sufficient to choose an optimal treatment. More information will usually have to be collected to complete the treatment selection stage. Similarly, the diagnostic label does not provide enough information to direct psychotherapists in the treatment evaluation stage. In the evaluation stage psychotherapists often rely on formal tests or behavioral measures such as diaries that record the frequency of panic attacks (for panic disorder patients, for example), rituals performed (for obsessive-compulsive patients), or participation in feared social interactions (for social phobics). Many psychotherapists also use more formal psychological tests to evaluate the overall emotional functioning of a client.

THE USE OF PSYCHOLOGICAL TESTS

Many psychotherapists rely on formal psychological tests and questionnaires to help in making treatment decisions. Others limit their use to those directly relevant to the patient's presenting complaint. Only psychotherapists who have received formal training in psychometric theory and test interpretation should use formal psychological tests. Others could refer for psychological testing when needed. In later sections we provide examples of how test profiles can improve treatment planning.

TABLE 2: **DEMOGRAPHIC AND CLINICAL VARIABLES ASSOCIATED WITH ANXIETY DISORDERS**

	Mean Age of Onset[a]	Prevalence per 100 Population[c]	Sex Ratio[a]	Familial Pattern	Reliability of Diagnosis[d]	Sodium Lactate Reaction	Anti-depressant Response	Complications
Simple Phobia	varies widely	2.5	F > M	high	.47	no	no	GAD
Social Phobia	16 (9)[b]	1.5	F = M	unknown	.77	no	no	depression d & a[f] avoidant pd[g]
Panic Disorder	27 (12)	3	F = M	high	.69	yes	yes	depression
Agora-phobia	26 (9)	6	F > M	high	.85	yes	yes	depression avoidant and dependent pd[g] d & a[f]
Generalized Anxiety Disorder	23 (12)	3	F = M	low	.47	no	no	other anxiety disorders

	Mean Age of Onset[a]	Prevalence per 100 Population[c]	Sex Ratio[a]	Familial Pattern	Reliability of Diagnosis[d]	Sodium Lactate Reaction	Anti-depressant Response	Complications
Obsessive-Compulsive Disorder	26 (15)		F > M	high	.66	no	sometimes	depression other anxiety disorders compulsive pd[g]
Post-Traumatic Stress Disorder	varies widely	varies	varies	low	.86[e]	no	sometimes	depression d & a[f]

a Thyer, Parrish, et al. (1985).
b Numbers in parentheses beside ages refer to standard deviations.
c Reich (1986).
d DiNardo et al. (1983).
e Blanchard et al. (1986).
f d & a = drug or alcohol abuse
g pd = personality disorder

5

The Life History Questionnaire. This questionnaire (Lazarus, 1976) elicits information on general problem areas, the patient's self-concept, the degree of distress, personal assets, and life history.

The Beck Depression Inventory. Depression is such a common co-existing or secondary problem to anxiety disorders that anxiety disorder patients should be routinely screened for the presence of depression. The Beck Depression Inventory (BDI) is the most frequently used measure of depression (Beck et al., 1961); it is now published by the Psychological Corporation. It assesses 21 symptoms including pessimism, sense of failure, dissatisfaction, self-accusations, suicidal ideas, indecisiveness, and somatic preoccupation. Psychotherapists may find items dealing with cognitive factors especially helpful for identifying demoralization secondary to the anxiety disorder, and the items dealing with vegetative symptoms such as loss of appetite, weight loss, and loss of libido can be suggestive of primary depression.

The BDI is either self-administered (10-15 minutes) or read to the patient. Each item has four or five possible responses, and each response is weighted between 0 and 3. Total scores range from 0 to 63.

Other Measures. The use of global personality measures such as the MMPI or projective testing are not usually necessary. These tests may, however, be helpful if the initial screening yields ambiguous or complicated findings and more information about the patient is desired. Behavioral diaries (Michelson, 1987) can be useful as diagnostic and treatment evaluation devices.

Table 3 (p. 7) displays average scores on commonly used assessment tools obtained by patients in various diagnostic categories. Table 3 contains scores from the BDI, the Fear Questionnaire (FQ) (Marks & Matthews, 1979), and the State-Trait Anxiety Inventory, Trait version (STAI) (Spielberger, Gorsuch, & Lushene, 1970). The FQ is a common assessment tool for social phobics and agoraphobics and is described in detail in the section entitled "Obsessive-Compulsive Disorders" (pp. 35-43). The STAI is commonly used to assess trait anxiety. Although we do not describe it in detail in the following sections,

**TABLE 3: SAMPLE ASSESSMENT SCORES
FOR ANXIETY DISORDERS**

	BDI[a] Scores	FQ (Social) (Subscale)	FQ (Agoraphobia) (Subscale)	STAI[a] (Trait)
Simple Phobia	15 (9)	8	9	43 (36) 41[b]
Social Phobia	12 (9)	34	6	54 (43) 51[b]
Panic Disorder	11 (18)	13	10	51 (49)
Agoraphobia	16 (17)	15	22	53 (51) 57[b]
General Anxiety Disorder	13 (23)	10	6	50 (63)
Obsessive-Compulsive Disorder	24 (25)	21	10	60 (63)
Post-Traumatic Stress Disorder	25[c]			54[c]

Note: Except as noted, all scores are from Barlow et al. (1986).

[a] Numbers in parentheses are from Turner, McCann, et al. (1986).
[b] From Cameron et al. (1986).
[c] From Fairbanks, Keane, and Malloy (1983).

its scores are listed here to provide another scale for comparison of the anxiety disorders.

OVERVIEW OF TREATMENT TECHNIQUES

This guide deals primarily with diagnosing anxiety disorders and selecting treatment. Although we do not provide comprehensive details about how to implement treatment techniques, this section does give an overview of treatment techniques commonly used for anxiety disorders with references for training materials. Readers are advised to acquire supervised training in the use of each of these techniques before implementing them.

Psychological treatment procedures can be divided into three general categories according to whether they address physiological (internal bodily reactions), cognitive/thinking, or interpersonal/environmental features of anxiety. No technique deals solely with one dimension, and our grouping is based on which factor seems to be primary in each of them.

Most of the therapeutic strategies suggested in this monograph have been developed out of the cognitive, behavioral, or pharmacological models because these have yielded the vast majority of process and outcome studies dealing with anxiety in the last 15 years (Sweet, Giles, & Young, 1987). Although psychotherapists may supplement these techniques by drawing on other therapeutic orientations, a detailed review of treatment manuals and outcome studies suggests that anxiety disorders are most effectively treated by using the cognitive, behavioral, or pharmacological models.

Physiological Techniques. For many patients anxiety has a strong physiological or bodily component, often described as tension. Several relaxation procedures have been developed to reduce body tension, with progressive muscle relaxation (PMR) the most widely used (Bernstein & Borkovec, 1974). In PMR the patient achieves total body relaxation by tensing and relaxing various groups of muscles in a systematic order often beginning with the feet and moving upward through the legs and abdomen to the shoulders, neck, and arms. PMR is also a primary ingredient for a number of other relaxation-based procedures such as systematic desensitization (Wolpe, 1982), in which the psychotherapist teaches patients deep muscle relaxation, then has them imagine scenes related to their phobia while in this state of relaxation. The imagined scenes are presented in a hierarchy from least to most fearful. Other techniques such as self-control desensitization and anxiety management training and other relaxation-based techniques also incorporate relaxation training with cognitive and interpersonal strategies (Barrios & Shigetomi, 1979; Woolfolk & Lehrer, 1984).

Flooding (Wolpe, 1982) is another technique that reduces physiological features of anxiety. Prolonged exposure to the feared situation allows extinction to gradually reduce the degree of anxiety. The exposure is often carried out in the patient's imagination before moving to the real situation. When flooding was first described there was some concern that it would cause psychiatric casualties because it requires prolonged exposure to the feared situation with a high degree of anxiety. However, the clinical and research literature indicate that psychiatric casualties due to this procedure are rare (Shipley & Boudewyns, 1980).

Cognitive Techniques. According to cognitive theories, patients can modify their dysfunctional anxiety reactions by modifying their thoughts. One popular cognitive technique involves changing irrational or unproductive beliefs. This treatment model, developed by Ellis (Whalen, DiGiuseppe, & Wessler, 1980), is called Rational Emotive Therapy (RET). Ellis created an A-B-C model to describe how irrational thoughts might produce anxiety. In this model, activating events (A) are interpreted erroneously through dysfunctional beliefs (B) leading to unproductive consequences such as anxiety or behavioral avoidance (C). Ellis has identified 11 common irrational beliefs such as the demand that one must be perfect in all activities one performs, or the demand that one must be loved and approved by all persons. RET treatment proceeds by debunking and removing these irrational beliefs.

Beck and Emery (1985) present a similar method of altering thoughts. Beck, however, emphasizes the processes of thinking more than the content of the unproductive beliefs. For example, in Beck's model, it might be seen as a case of overgeneralized thinking if a single social rejection causes a person to shy away from other social opportunities. Beck and his associates place more emphasis on developing a positive and collaborative relationship with their patients than does Ellis, and they have presented more supportive outcome data.

Although the cognitive therapies may have a different theoretical base than behavior therapy, the two schools often employ identical or similar techniques. For example, Ellis would use systematic desensitization with certain patients. Beck incorporates many behavioral activities such as graduated exposure or gradual approximation in the treatment of anxiety (Beck & Emery, 1985).

Thought stopping is a cognitive technique (Wolpe, 1982) that involves getting rid of thoughts rather than changing the content of specific thoughts. Symptom-inducing thoughts can be interrupted through physical activities or cognitive activities which divert attention.

Guided imagery may also be used as a cognitive strategy to control or reduce anxiety. During guided imagery (Lazarus, 1976) the patient practices the successful imaginal rehearsal of difficult social situations. Another technique known as paradoxical intention (Michelson &

Ascher, 1984) involves reducing anticipatory anxiety by consciously trying to create the feared anxiety.

Interpersonal/Environmental Techniques. Anxiety may seriously interfere with patients' interactions with the world around them and with other people. One of the most commonly used techniques to reduce interpersonal components of anxiety is assertiveness training (Lange & Jakubowski, 1975). In the popular perception, assertiveness means "standing up for your rights." Wolpe (1982), however, defines assertiveness as the appropriate interpersonal expression of any emotion which is incompatible with anxiety. Consequently, Wolpe's procedures involve more broad-spectrum social skills training. Making friends, carrying on conversations, and resolving conflicts are included within Wolpe's definition of assertiveness training.

Another technique that focuses on changing the patient's relationship with the environment is response prevention (Steketee & Foa, 1985). Response prevention is used to prevent unproductive rituals or behavior linked to anxiety reduction, especially with obsessive-compulsive disorders (see commentary in the section entitled "Obsessive-Compulsive Disorders," pp. 35-43).

Graduated exposure is a technique by which patients gradually expose themselves to a feared situation. This may involve confronting an object, as in simple phobias, or going to places of perceived danger, as in panic disorder or agoraphobia (Barlow & Waddell, 1985). In addition, Weekes (1976, 1984), Zane and Milt (1984), and Neuman (1985) have all developed treatments that contain elements of graduated exposure. For example, during graduated exposure treatments, patients will deliberately place themselves in locations or situations that have previously elicited panic attacks. Furthermore, they are taught various techniques such as relaxation, somatic relabeling, or attention diversion to reduce the likelihood or severity of the panic attack. Patients are required to stay in the situation and not to leave even if they experience another panic attack. Consequently, they can break the chain between panic and avoidance of public places. Perhaps nowhere does the line between physiological, cognitive, and motoric interventions become more blurred than with graduated exposure, where cognitions are modified to change physiological reactions and increase tolerance of the phobic situation.

SIMPLE PHOBIAS

Simple or specific phobias are characterized by persistent irrational fears and avoidance of specific situations or objects. This category does not include social phobias or agoraphobias. Blood-injury-illness (BII) phobias are classified under simple phobias within the *DSM-III-R*, although they differ sufficiently from other simple phobias to require unique treatment procedures and probably deserve a separate diagnostic category (Thyer, Himle, & Curtis, 1985). These are discussed in a separate section entitled "Blood, Injury, and Illness Phobias," page 16.

The age of onset for simple phobias varies considerably, ranging from childhood through adulthood. About two-thirds of simple phobias start from a direct trauma or a series of minor traumas. Others occur through observing another person being harmed or through misinformation. The sex ratio of simple phobias would be equal except that women far exceed men in their frequency of small animal phobias.

As a group, simple phobias are less severe and debilitating than other anxiety disorders and usually do not severely limit social or occupational activities. Nevertheless, many patients with simple phobia have other concurrent anxiety disorders that in combination can be debilitating.

DIFFERENTIAL DIAGNOSIS

Usually the self-report of the patient will be sufficient to assess the extent of the phobia. If the feared object is readily available in the natural environment, then a behavioral avoidance test may be used. The psychotherapist can use a fear thermometer (ranking anxiety on a scale of 0 to 10 with 0 = "no anxiety" and 10 = "extreme anxiety") to assess the degree of anxiety.

Often simple phobias appear within a package of multiple phobias. Usually these multiple phobias develop through generalization from the original trauma. The patient who appears with multiple phobias often can identify a common theme for all the different phobias. For example, a patient involved in a vehicular accident may develop a fear of riding in vehicles, or of certain sounds associated with the operation of vehicles.

Simple phobias differ from post-traumatic stress disorder in that the phobic patient does not re-experience the event through intrusive recollections or flashbacks and does not have the extreme denial of emotional upset. The Fear Survey Schedule (Wolpe & Lang, 1969) can help to determine the degree of generalization or the extent of multiple phobias.

Simple phobias sometimes mask or co-exist with other serious mental disorders. A distinction should be made between a real phobia, which masks or co-exists with other problems, and a pseudophobia, which is invented for an ulterior motive. Patients may "test" the psychotherapist's trustworthiness and competence by initially presenting a less threatening aspect of their pathology such as a simple phobia. A thorough social and clinical history and mental status check should identify the patient with a "pseudophobia." The "pseudophobic" patient will not show the degree of upset and avoidance found with real phobias and will gradually shift the contents of conversation to more clinically relevant areas.

TREATMENTS FOR SIMPLE PHOBIAS

A variety of behavioral procedures have been endorsed for treatment of simple phobias including, among others, systematic desensitization, *in vivo* desensitization, implosive therapy, flooding, reinforced practice, modeling (including participant and covert modeling), and cognitive therapy with exposure. We have described some of these treatments briefly in the section entitled "Introduction" (pp. 1-10). To date, none of these techniques have been shown to be superior to the others, although cognitive therapy without exposure may be inferior. All other strategies can reduce simple phobias with a high degree of success.

No definitive research exists to predict which features of a simple phobia can best guide treatment selection from this list of possible approaches. Based on the limited literature, we prefer to select treatments on the basis of the origin of the phobia or on the ability of the patient to create imagery to evoke emotions. Although Schwartz, Davidson, and Coleman (1978) have discussed treatment selection based on mode of symptom response to the phobia (physiological, behavioral, cognitive), the research support for this as a routine approach to treatment selection is limited.

Origin of Phobias. We recommend following Wolpe's (1981, 1982) tailoring of treatments for simple phobias according to their origin. Wolpe identified two modes of phobia onset: classical conditioning and cognitive misinformation. Wolpe believes that the different modes of onset warrant different treatment procedures. According to Wolpe, a treatment such as systematic desensitization that is designed for the deconditioning of anxiety would not have much effect on phobic responses that require cognitive solutions.

There is no formal method of determining the mode of onset. Psychotherapists generally can inquire about the origin of the fear and whether the original situation was perceived as being dangerous and warranting fear. For example, a phobia of thunderstorms that developed from being caught in a serious flood or tornado would differ from one that developed out of false ideas concerning the dangers of thunderstorms. Of course, many phobias do not follow one single traumatic event but result from numerous mini-traumas or anxiety provoking experiences. Similarly, the acquisition of false beliefs does not always occur through direct education. Sometimes phobics have inferred false information about the harmfulness of thunderstorms or spiders, for example, by observing the reactions of parents or others.

Some simple phobias may be based on both direct trauma and false information. In such cases, both cognitive correction and relaxation training may be required. Airplane flight phobias are a common example of multiple causation. Although misconceptions about the safety factor in flying appear to most commonly cause flight phobias, unpleasant experiences while flying, such as nausea or flight sickness during a rough flight, may cause or aggravate other phobias.

Some research supports this distinction between phobias based on trauma and phobias based on false information. Wolpe's (1981) anecdotal retrospective study supported his conclusions. Also, Öst (1985) reported success with treating phobics differently according to mode of acquisition (phobias acquired vicariously were considered cognitively acquired phobias). The sample, however, included social phobics, dental and blood phobics, and agoraphobics, as well as simple phobics, so it is unclear how his results would apply to simple phobias only. Although patients with conditioned fears did not respond differently to treatments (exposure, *in vivo* desensitization,

13

or applied relaxation), those patients with cognitively based fears progressed better with the cognitive treatment modalities (self-instructional training or fading).

Systematic desensitization and its variations are the preferred treatments with conditioned phobias. Patients with multiple phobias should have a separate hierarchy created for each phobia unless the behavioral analysis shows an underlying theme or connection among the apparently different fears.

Although systematic desensitization involving progressive muscle relaxation (PMR) is the treatment of choice, relaxation methods other than PMR can be used. Some patients have had prior experience or interest in self-hypnosis, meditation, yoga, or biofeedback enhanced relaxation. Wolpe (1982) also described patients who used Kung-Fu, motoric exercises, or reading to inhibit anxiety. These methods of inducing relaxation work just as effectively as PMR for individual patients.

In the absence of patient preferences, however, we prefer PMR because it has a relatively low rate of negative side-effects. More patients report transient anxiety effects during the practice of meditation than during the practice of PMR probably because of the increased somatic awareness common to these related states. Lehrer and Woolfolk (1984) believe that these anxiety reactions are less common in PMR because it more directly lowers heart rate and muscle tension.

Ability to Utilize Imagery. A few patients cannot create imagery that is vivid enough for imaginal systematic desensitization to work effectively. They may have trouble evoking the images or be unable to create strong emotions out of the images. Strategies are available to increase the effectiveness of imagery (Wolpe, 1982), but if these fail, the psychotherapist could shift to *in vivo* desensitization or flooding.

Mode of Response. Another perspective on treatment selection is based on the predominant response system, or the modified "specific-effects" hypothesis. We have reviewed the literature and the data on this perspective and do not recommend it as a routine approach for selecting treatments for simple phobias. According to this hypothesis, all relaxation techniques produce a general relaxation response. In addition, specific treatments have specific effects superimposed upon the general relaxation state. For example, cognitive treatments are more likely to reduce cognitive anxiety, somatic treatments are more likely to reduce somatic or physiological anxiety, and behavioral treatments are more likely to reduce behavioral symptoms of anxiety such as avoidance (Schwartz et al., 1978).

Although this schema has face appeal, several problems argue against its routine application in clinical practice. First, treatments cannot be neatly categorized as cognitive, somatic, or behavioral. Systematic desensitization, for example, contains the somatic element of progressive muscle relaxation, but it also includes cognitive elements by increasing expectancy of improvement and even behavioral elements when exposure to the objects in fantasy may transfer to real-life exposure.

Also, the mode of response procedure for choosing treatments may produce contradictory results with the mode of acquisition schema. Some evidence suggests that classically conditioned phobias are more likely to produce physiological arousal than phobias acquired through misinformation (Öst & Hugdahl, 1981). Furthermore, psychotherapists will not always be able to classify patients as behavioral, cognitive, or physiological responders because response measures may not be sensitive to actual internal states. Physiological responses are especially difficult to measure unless psychotherapists have access to extensive recording equipment.

Finally, the evidence from outcome studies for this degree of treatment specificity has been inconsistent. For example, Öst, Johansson, and Jerremalm (1982) found that exposure was most effective with behavioral responders, while relaxation produced better outcomes with physiological responders among claustrophobia patients. Later, however, Jerremalm, Johansson, and Öst (1986a) failed to find differential effectiveness for a cognitive over a relaxation-based treatment for differential responders suffering from dental anxiety.

In the final analysis, the research data do not support the differential application of treatments based on the predominant mode of response. Nonetheless, psychotherapists may find individual clients who demonstrate extreme cognitive, behavioral, or physiological responses and may elect to apply differential treatments on a case-by-case basis.

15

BLOOD, INJURY, AND ILLNESS PHOBIAS

Blood, injury, and illness (BII) phobias differ so much from simple phobias that we believe they warrant a separate diagnostic classification. Blood, injury, and illness phobias are classified together because they have a similar sex distribution and diphasic response. That is, the patient first feels a typical phobic anxiety state characterized by physiological arousal, cognitions of fear, and avoidance. These reactions are followed by a second phase characterized by a decrease in physiological arousal (e.g., heart rate, blood pressure) and eventually feelings of faintness. Fainting often does occur in BII, whereas fainting does not occur in other simple phobias.

Most (50% to 75%) patients acquire BII phobias through direct experiences. The sex distribution is equal between men and women. Three-fifths of BII patients also have other *DSM-III-R* diagnoses, primarily anxiety or depression.

Evidence from one controlled study (Öst & Sterner, 1987) and several case reports supports a diphasic treatment plan for BII. Psychotherapists should first teach the patient relaxation techniques (theoretically any relaxation procedure should work). Patients should apply these relaxation skills at the onset of the first phase (an increase in blood pressure or heart rate). If this intervention is successful, then the second phase of the disorder will not occur. If the relaxation response does not reduce anxiety and the second phase does occur, patients can apply tension or anger-arousing techniques to counteract the second phase (Öst & Sterner, 1987). The outcome for the diphasic treatment is good.

SOCIAL PHOBIAS

Michelle is a 20-year-old secretary from a working class family who has a good paying job with a prestigious law firm. She reported feeling tense at work, and she described a strong desire to succeed on the job and to please her boss. One day at work she heard some of the other secretaries making sarcastic comments about her work behind her back. Afterwards Michelle became very timid and anxious around them and often stammered when she spoke. She now avoids them whenever possible. Michelle makes careless mistakes in her work whenever others are near her. Currently she is looking for a different job where she can feel more comfortable.

Michelle has a social phobia. The *DSM-III-R* defines social phobias as "a persistent fear of one or more situations (the social phobic situations) in which the person is exposed to possible scrutiny by others and fears that he or she may do something or act in a way that will be humiliating or embarrassing" (p. 241). Common examples of social phobias include a fear of being unable to talk in public, of choking on food when eating in front of others, of being unable to urinate in a public lavatory, or of having a hand tremble when writing in the presence of others. In some cases, the social phobia may be generalized to most social situations and include a fear of saying foolish things or of not being able to answer questions. A social phobia can greatly impair a patient's social life and occupational adjustment.

Marked anticipatory anxiety occurs when people suffering from this phobia are faced with the necessity of entering the feared situation. Whenever possible, they will avoid the situations, but if they are forced to endure it, they will experience intense immediate anxiety, as well as fears that others will detect signs of their discomfort. A vicious cycle often ensues in which the anxiety impairs their performance, leading to increased efforts to avoid the situation. One of the *DSM-III-R* criteria for this classification is that the fear may not be due to another psychiatric disorder. Social fear caused by paranoia, for example, is not a social phobia.

Although the age of onset for social phobia varies considerably, it commonly begins in the late teens or early adulthood (as in the case of Michelle), when the individual begins to separate from the family of origin. The onset is often triggered by a direct trauma or a series of minitraumas. It is equally prevalent in men and women. The course of the disorder is often chronic; it rarely dissipates without treatment. Social phobics have a high incidence of negative self-statements or irrational beliefs.

By the time treatment is sought, social phobics often have added more problems to their lives. Turner, Beidel, et al. (1986) found that 46% of social phobics used alcohol to reduce anxiety in social settings and 52% used antianxiety drugs before entering social settings. Many patients in alcohol treatment facilities have a social phobia or an avoidant personality disorder that appears to pre-date the alcohol disorder. Turner, Beidel, et al. (1986) also found that 33% of their sample had simple phobias (mostly fear of heights or small animals). More than 33% of the patients had a history of depression.

DIFFERENTIAL DIAGNOSIS

Sometimes it is difficult to distinguish social phobias from panic disorders (agoraphobia). For example, both social phobics and panic disorder patients may report fears of going to restaurants, theaters, and social events. The distinction is that social phobics have a fear of being with other people, whereas agoraphobics fear their own spontaneous panic attacks. Although agoraphobics may fear embarrassment or scrutiny during a panic attack, the embarrassment is limited to actions that may occur during the panic attack and does not generalize to other social situations. These and other differences are shown in Table 4 (p. 19).

Psychotherapists must distinguish social phobias from schizoid and avoidant personality disorders. Both social phobics and schizoid personality disorder patients avoid social contact. Social phobics, however, would like to have social contacts, but fear blocks their interactions with others. The person with a schizoid personality disorder has no interest in others, lacks feelings of warmth and empathy, and is indifferent to praise or criticism from others.

It can also be difficult to distinguish social phobia from avoidant personality disorder. Some investigators consider avoidant personality disorder to be a more perva-sive social fear, whereas social phobia is restricted to a few highly specific social fears such as dating, public speaking, and eating in public. Turner, Beidel, et al. (1986) suggest that avoidant personality disorders are dis-tinguishable from social phobias because persons with social phobias have better social skills. According to them, the avoidant personality disorder patient requires social skills training, whereas the social phobic must be treated first with anxiety reduction techniques (systematic desensitization, anxiety management training, cognitive restructuring, etc.). Once the fear level is reduced, the therapist can assess the phobic's level of social skills and determine the need for more treatment.

TABLE 4: DIFFERENCES BETWEEN SOCIAL PHOBIA AND AGORAPHOBIA

Feature	Social Phobia	Agoraphobia
	Symptom Differences	
Situations Avoided	parties, social gatherings, restaurants, theaters, and so on	places where panic attacks have happened before or where they might happen
Response	anticipatory anxiety, general anxiety	anticipatory anxiety; panic
Anticipatory Thoughts	Others will laugh at me; I will humiliate myself.	I will die; I will faint; No one will help me.
Moderating Circumstances	presence of significant others	presence of significant others
Course	mostly static	fluctuates
Complications	alcohol, drug abuse; depression; simple phobias	alcohol, drug abuse; depression; simple phobias; GAD symptoms
	Demographic Features	
Age of Onset	19 (average)	26 (average)
Sex Ratio	F = M	F>M
	Physiological Differences	
Sodium Lactate Response	low	high
Antidepressant Response	low	high

Psychological tests such as the Millon Clinical Multi-axial Inventory may aid in the understanding of social phobia. This inventory includes 20 subscales, eight of which define various long-term personality styles. Scale 2 defines the Avoidant Personality Style. A profile in which the Anxiety Scale and the Avoidant Personality Scale are both elevated might describe a social phobia in an avoidant personality disorder, but an elevated Anxiety

ne absence of any personality style scale eleva-
suggest a social phobia.

DSM-III-R does not recognize performance anxi-
ach as public speaking anxiety or athletic perform-
anxiety as specific or separate diagnostic categories.
M ny of these performance anxieties are probably better
understood and treated as apparent social phobias. At
times the social aspects of performance anxiety may be
subtle. For example, sexual performance anxiety may be
due to a fear of rejection, overconcern about performance, or fear of humiliation by a partner. A fear of dis-
appointing one's parents or of lowered status in peer relationships may cause test anxiety.

TREATMENTS FOR SOCIAL PHOBIAS

Because it is a relatively new category of disorder,
few treatment studies are available on social phobias.
The most relevant research has been conducted with patients having public speaking anxiety, dating anxiety, and
other forms of anxiety in social situations. Many of the
patients in these research projects could have met the
DSM-III-R criteria for social phobia. It is unclear, however, how many of these participants could also have been
diagnosed as having avoidant personality disorders,
general anxiety disorders, or depression diagnoses, or how
many had subclinical levels of fear. Consequently, the
earlier research on social anxiety may not necessarily generalize to the diagnosis of and treatment selection for
social phobias.

Studies of treatment effectiveness with social phobias
and pre-*DSM-III* studies of social anxiety indicate that
treatments such as Rational Emotive Therapy, *in vivo* exposure, or one of many relaxation-based treatments may
be effective in treating social phobias. Many relaxation-
based programs have been used for the treatment of social, general, and performance anxieties. These programs
are highly similar, and none appears to have superiority
(Barrios & Shigetomi, 1979). As with simple phobias,
researchers have tried to develop treatment specificity for
social phobias. According to the multiprocess theory of
relaxation and related states, different treatment strategies should impact differently depending on whether they
target the cognitive, physiological, or behavioral components of the anxiety. Unfortunately, the studies of

treatment specificity with social phobias are contradictory and full of methodological problems.

A study by Turner and Beidel (1985) identified two subtypes of social anxiety patients who differed primarily in level of physiological reactivity. The first category consisted of patients with negative thought patterns and high physiological reactivity. The second category consisted of patients who had negative thoughts but low physiological reactivity. A subsequent study dividing subjects into cognitive and physiological reactors failed to find differential treatment effectiveness (Jerremalm, Johansson, & Öst, 1986b). These authors, however, did not classify social phobics in exactly the same manner as did Turner and Beidel.

Öst, Jerremalm, and Johansson (1981) divided social phobics into behavioral or physiological reactors and found that the treatment matched to subject response mode was more effective than unmatched treatments. Later, McCann, Woolfolk, and Lehrer (1987) found that rational restructuring led to a greater decrease in cognitive anxiety, behavioral rehearsal led to a greater improvement in behavioral measures of social anxiety, but progressive muscle relaxation failed to demonstrate superiority with autonomic measures of anxiety.

These and other outcome studies with treatment mode specificity have failed to produce consistent results. This may be due, in part, to the differing schemas that authors have used for categorizing social phobias according to social skills, cognitive features, or physiological reactivity. We suggest that psychotherapists treat whatever response mode of the patient appears dysfunctional, starting with the most dysfunctional mode. Treatment effects may generalize into other response modes, but if the generalization is not complete, the next most dysfunctional response mode can then be addressed.

For example, the psychotherapist treating Michelle, described in the opening vignette, may learn that she has an excessive need to seek the approval of others. At the time of the assessment, she reports little physiological reactivity when in the phobic situation. She appears to be cooperative and eager to work on her problem. However, if her scores on a measure of assertiveness indicate that she is not assertive and further questioning about her interactions with others supports this finding, treatment should start with altering her dysfunctional beliefs about pleasing others. Specific skill training on the fundamentals of assertiveness may also be helpful.

The negative cognitions of social phobics can be assessed through interviewing or reviewing the patient's responses on the Life History Questionnaire. The interviewer can look for irrational beliefs or dysfunctional thinking styles (Beck & Emery, 1985) that are possible mediators of anxiety.

Psychotherapists can assess the patient's social skills by noticing how the patient relates with them or with family members in the sessions, or by asking the patient to describe social interactions. Patients can also be assessed through the use of self-report assertiveness or social skills inventories. Sometimes patients report good social skills on self-report inventories, but then display rudeness, excessive shyness, inconsiderateness, or other inappropriate behaviors with the interviewer or family members. Such discrepancies between actual behaviors and self-report scores suggest that such patients do not have an accurate view of their own behaviors. Treatment should address these "blind spots."

Physiological reactivity is harder to measure. Although research laboratories use elaborate equipment to measure heart rate or blood pressure in structured testing situations, most psychotherapists do not own this equipment. Furthermore, some researchers question the usefulness of being able to monitor only one or two physiological measures. When sophisticated equipment is not available, the psychotherapist must rely on the self-report of the patient.

PHARMACOLOGICAL TREATMENTS

Although pharmacological treatments show some promise with social anxiety, the data have not yet convinced us to prefer pharmacological over behavioral treatments. Some case studies and one uncontrolled study suggest that monoamine oxidase inhibitors may benefit social phobics (Liebowitz et al., 1985). Also, case studies and reports of uncontrolled studies claim that beta-adrenergic blockers (such as propranolol) reduce performance anxiety for speakers and musicians as well as those having more well-defined social phobias. There is at least one report that diazepam (Valium) can reduce public speaking anxiety when administered prior to the speech. The long-term effects of diazepam for this purpose have not been evaluated. Tricyclic antidepressants have not proven effective in treating social phobias (see review by Liebowitz et al., 1987).

Currently, we recommend first offering a behavioral treatment program. The program should be tailored to the needs of the patient by addressing the behavioral, physiological, or cognitive deficiencies as assessed by the psychotherapist. Systematic or self-control desensitization should be used for social phobics whose fear appears to be based on direct conditioning. In addition, cognitive restructuring is usually indicated because most socially anxious persons have some negative thoughts. The need for social skills training depends on the assessment. Pharmacological options can be used if the patient refuses to accept the behavioral program or expresses a preference to try medication first. Nonresponders to psychotherapy can, of course, be referred for pharmacological interventions, and vice versa.

A CASE VIGNETTE

Harriet is a 24-year-old graduate student in experimental psychology who is conscientious and always tries to be thoroughly prepared. She often studies her notes until she has practically memorized them. Harriet's study time is so extensive she can afford almost no social life. Still, she has found herself "worked up" over her grades. She described nervous feelings in her stomach, and she was unable to relax. According to her Life History Questionnaire, she has been this way ever since she was a sophomore in college. One day Harriet experienced a very sudden and intense nervousness while presenting a lecture on theories of emotion to one of her graduate classes. Because of other demands on her time, she had not been able to prepare adequately. She worried about the comments and questions of the other class members and was quick to interpret them as criticisms. Although she got a grade of "B" for the lecture, she thought that the instructor was frowning and grimacing during the lecture and really did not like her presentation. Since that time, she has assiduously tried to avoid giving class presentations.

Diagnosis and Treatment Recommendations

Diagnosis. Axis I: Social Phobia
                       Probable Generalized Anxiety Disorder
              Axis II: Not Sufficient Information

Treatment Plan. Because Harriet has high self-reported physiological arousal, and because the fear of public speaking started with one specific situation, we would use a desensitization procedure. She probably also has generalized anxiety disorder, so we would choose self-control desensitization, which theoretically can be applied to a wide range of anxiety producing situations. Dysfunctional cognitions related to public speaking and generalized anxiety need to be assessed through interviews to determine whether treatment should include a cognitive component, along with more information about her social skills to indicate whether training in this area would be helpful.

PANIC ATTACKS AND AGORAPHOBIA

Jill is an 18-year-old freshman college student who came to the Counseling Service complaining of severe anxiety. She reported sudden heart palpitations, nervousness, hyperventilation, and fear of "going crazy." She described the first episode in great detail. Since then, she has had several such "anxiety" episodes in the last month. She is now afraid of going outside without her boyfriend for fear of having another attack. A medical examination failed to find any physical reasons for her attacks.

Jill has a panic disorder. This is a complicated, confusing, and debilitating psychiatric disorder. Often, panic disorders lead to agoraphobia, or the fear of going away from places of safety. In the *DSM-III*, agoraphobia and panic disorder were considered separate diagnoses. The *DSM-III-R*, however, considers agoraphobia as a complication of panic disorders. Typically, persons having agoraphobia proceed through two stages of development: panic attacks and then phobic avoidance or the fear of being away from places of safety.

The *DSM-III-R* established several criteria for the diagnosis of panic disorder. The panic attack must be spontaneous (not in the presence of life-endangering situations or phobic stimuli). Also, it requires that the patient experience at least four attacks in a 4-week period and that the attacks include at least 4 out of 12 possible symptoms. The possible symptoms include an increase in blood pressure, dizziness, chest pains, tachycardia, trouble breathing, trouble swallowing, paresthesia (tingling in hands or feet), hot or cold flashes, sweating, faintness, trembling, and shaking. The physical sensations differ so much from other physical states that patients often feel unreal or like they are "going crazy." Some patients may have other less common symptoms. Physiological measures of panic disorder patients verify the sudden onset and intensity of the panic attack.

The designation of four panic attacks within a 4-week period is admittedly arbitrary. These requirements were established because infrequent panic attacks occur in other diagnostic categories, and about one-third of nonpsychiatric persons experience at least one panic attack in a year. Most people, however, do not have repeated panic attacks and do not develop fear of future panic attacks.

The second phase in the development of agoraphobia is the phobic avoidance. Agoraphobic patients fear that panic attacks will recur, and consequently they restrict their movements to places such as their home, or they will go out only in the presence of a trusted person such as a spouse. Although the phobic avoidance could occur immediately after the first panic attack, the avoidance phase most often develops after repeated panic attacks over a period of months or years.

Panic disorders usually emerge between the ages of 16 and 35. Most studies report that a higher number of women than men are affected, usually by a 3:1 ratio, although this ratio may be misleading. Many male patients in alcohol treatment facilities report that they started drinking to "medicate" themselves against their anxiety and panic symptoms. If this is true, then the actual sex ratio may be more equal, with many male alcoholics having hidden panic disorders. Despite numerous exceptions, male agoraphobics tend to succumb to phobic avoidance less than women do. The sex role expectations of men to leave the house and earn a living may place more social pressure on men to minimize phobic avoidance.

Although panic disorders are chronic, there may be periods of remission for no apparent reason and periods in which the symptoms are worse. Often the periods of remission are characterized by depression or free-floating anxiety.

There is some speculation that separation anxiety in children and dependent or avoidant personality features in adults predispose persons to the disorder, but these speculations do not have clear empirical support (Marks, 1987). A family history of panic disorder or depression increases the likelihood of developing the disorder. The initial panic attack usually occurs after a loss (e.g., death or divorce) or a major life change (e.g., birth of a child).

COMBINING PANIC DISORDER AND AGORAPHOBIA

The *DSM-III* separated agoraphobia into two groups: agoraphobia with panic attacks, and agoraphobia without panic attacks. A third category, panic disorder, was also created. The *DSM-III-R* revised the *DSM-III* by classifying agoraphobia as a complication of the panic disorder. Agoraphobia without panic attacks is extremely rare and is listed as agoraphobia without history of panic disorder (see Table 1, p. 2).

The reclassification of panic disorders and agoraphobia makes sense from a diagnostic and treatment planning viewpoint because panic disorder and agoraphobia appear to be the same disorder at different levels of intensity, and not separate diagnostic entities. The age of onset and the description of the panic attacks of the two categories are identical. Furthermore, agoraphobic patients almost always claim that the panic preceded the phobic avoidance. Both panic disorder patients and agoraphobic patients typically develop "spontaneous" panic attacks in response to infusion of sodium lactate (an artificial means of inducing panic attacks), whereas persons without a history of panic attacks seldom show such a response (Sheehan, 1984).

Turner, S. L. Williams, et al. (1986) found that panic disorder patients were highly similar to agoraphobic patients in diagnostic features. They differed, however, in severity and number of complications. Agoraphobic patients, by definition, demonstrated more extensive phobic avoidance. Also, they were more interpersonally sensitive, more prone to alcohol abuse, experienced fewer periods of spontaneous remission, and described more symptoms oc-curring during the panic attacks. In summary, agora-phobic patients appeared to have a more chronic or more severe form of panic disorder.

Although some persons do not meet the *DSM-III-R* criteria for panic disorder because their panic attacks are not sufficiently frequent, they experience the same effect as those whose attacks can be diagnosed as panic disorder. That is, fear of an attack keeps the patients close to safe places, and they require the same treatment as diagnosa-ble panic disorder patients.

MEDICAL SCREENING OF PATIENTS
HAVING PANIC ATTACKS

A small minority of panic disorder patients have medi-cal conditions that mimic panic attacks. Although not recognized within the *DSM-III-R*, some writers have called this the "organic anxiety disorder." The physical symptoms of panic often lead these patients to believe they have a physical disorder, and most patients present-ing for treatment of anxiety disorders have already had numerous physical examinations and medical tests before seeking mental health treatment. Patients who come directly for mental health treatment for panic attacks without a physical screening should receive a medical evaluation before or during early phases of treatment. The medical examination should include a thyroid evaluation because thyroid disorders may mimic panic attacks.

The psychotherapist should request a medical re-evaluation in two situations. First, patients should be re-examined if they have atypical symptoms such as cloud-ing of consciousness, loss of intellectual functioning, fainting, strong feelings of derealization followed by aggression or verbal hostility, the onset of the panic that coincides with a specific physical problem, age of onset before 16 or after 40, and lack of positive family history for panic disorder, depression, or anxiety. Second, pa-tients should receive a medical re-examination if they fail to respond to standard psychological or pharmacological treatments.

The most common organic sources of anxiety include overuse of caffeine, and withdrawal from drugs (in-cluding over-the-counter nonprescription drugs and illicit drugs, such as marijuana or cocaine) and alcohol. Caffeine commonly causes or exacerbates anxiety and panic disorders, and people vary substantially in their tolerance. Although some can consume large quantities of caffeine with no ill effects, others react to the amount in one or two cups of coffee, tea, or other sources. For some patients the moderate use of caffeine may counter the anti-anxiety effects of prescription medication or relaxation exercises. Abrupt discontinuation of large amounts of caffeine can cause withdrawal symptoms including headaches, tachycardia, agitation, or panic attacks. Many panic disorder patients have discontinued caffeine intake on their own because they realized it increased their anxiety and frequency of panic attacks. Other patients may resist giving up caffeine because the withdrawal includes anxiety symptoms.

CO-EXISTING OR COMPLICATING DISORDERS

The diagnosis and treatment planning for panic disorders and agoraphobia can be difficult. Some clinicians distinguish between simple and complex agoraphobia. Simple agoraphobic patients only have panic attacks and phobic avoidance without other psychological problems. Complex agoraphobic patients have a wide range of other psychological problems such as marital problems, major depression, and avoidant or dependent features.

The distinction between simple and complex agoraphobia appears to have some validity. Between one-fourth and one-half of patients with agoraphobia have personality disorders, and the more severely symptomatic agoraphobic patients have more symptoms of personality disorders. The direction of causality is not clear: The severe panic and agoraphobic symptoms may predispose persons to develop personality disorder features, the personality disorder may predispose persons to panic symptoms, or a common underlying vulnerability may cause both disorders.

Major depression is also a common complication of panic disorder and agoraphobia. Although rates of depression vary slightly from study to study, about half of agoraphobic patients display significant depressive symptoms at the start of treatment. The psychotherapist needs to distinguish major depression from the demoralization likely to accompany any severe psychiatric or medical disorder; the withdrawal and social isolation caused by the agoraphobia may create loneliness and demoralization. Patients often are so pre-occupied with the panic attacks that they do not recognize the vegetative symptoms of depression as such and need to be asked about them directly or given the BDI, MMPI, or MCMI to ascertain whether they are present. A distinction also needs to be made between depression with panic attacks and panic disorder with depression. Patients with severe major depression commonly have panic attacks. The use of antidepressants may be indicated in cases of co-existing panic and major depression because the antidepressants can remedy both the depression and the panic.

The relationship between panic disorder and marital difficulties is controversial. Older theories held that agoraphobics had marital problems more often than nonagoraphobics - that the marital situation either created the panic disorder or kept the panic disorder patient dependent, and that marital therapy was needed. It also has been hypothesized that treating the agoraphobic may harm the marital relationship and that spouses (especially husbands) may sabotage the therapy program or become depressed themselves as patients become more assertive and less dependent. Recent studies, however, suggest that this is not necessarily typical. Although some panic disorder patients have poor marriages, and some husbands have an apparent co-dependency on their wives and resist change, most will support treatment (Barlow & Waddell, 1985). Treatment plans that incorporate spouses have become popular and have given therapists an opportunity to monitor marital relationships.

TREATMENTS FOR PANIC
DISORDERS AND AGORAPHOBIA

Few disorders require as much treatment flexibility and variation as panic disorders. Currently, two main models of treatment selection which have merit, the behavioral and the pharmacological, are being promoted. Of course, neither is a pure model. Many behavior therapists encourage their patients to use benzodiazepines in conjunction with behavior therapy, and pharmacotherapists often use behavioral techniques as an adjunct to medication. The initial treatment choice depends on the preferences of the patient and the therapist and the existence of concurrent psychiatric problems.

Because neither medication nor behavior therapy alone will succeed with all panic disorder patients, psychotherapists should consider both approaches in cases of incomplete response. It is best to inform patients at the onset about different treatment options because some will have strong, preconceived biases about certain treatments. Some may insist upon medication and have no desire to participate in a behavioral program involving exposure to the feared situation or panic, whereas others may refuse to take medications under any circumstances. Most patients, however, are open to considering treatment options. Panic patients generally have endured so many years of distress without relief from symptoms that they are relieved to find a therapist who can understand the disorder and discuss treatment options.

Usually we start treatment with a behavioral approach because it has a lower drop-out rate than the pharmacological approach. Also, clinical evidence suggests that it is easier to shift from a behavioral approach to a pharmacological approach than vice versa. Once relief from panic has been achieved by taking medication, these patients lose tolerance for the panic attacks that are an inevitable part of behavior therapy. Moreover, the skills learned in behavior therapy (such as graduated exposure and relaxation) are transferable to the medication program. We would, however, recommend a pharmacological approach first if the patient strongly preferred that modality, or if the patient evidenced concurrent severe major depression.

Core Approaches. Whatever the initial approach, we recommend starting treatment with an educational program and an assessment of the degree of disability. First, the psychotherapist should educate the patient about the nature of panic disorder. Typically patients are demoralized by the disorder and may have a great deal of self-blame. The educational program reduces self-blame by explaining that the panic attacks have a discernible basis, and that patients and their previous physicians have understandably not been able to identify or diagnose the attacks because of the bewildering array of symptoms that often present as panic disorder. In addition, the educational program should explain the possible treatment procedures. The procedures and outcome data concerning the various treatment procedures (behavioral and pharmacological) must be described accurately.

The educational program can be accomplished through bibliotherapy, discussions with the patient, questions and answers, contact with other panic disorder patients, and through educational tapes. Panic disorder patients are greatly relieved to learn that they are not crazy or malingerers, and that treatments are available for their disorder. Knapp and VandeCreek (1988) have recommended various valuable books. *Agoraphobia: A Clinical and Personal Account* (Clarke & Wardman, 1985), written by a former phobic, provides a very personalized description of the symptoms and treatment. Several excellent books have also been written by therapists, including *More Hope and Help for Your Nerves* (Weekes, 1984), *Fighting Fear* (Neuman, 1985), *Your Phobia* (Zane & Milt, 1984), and *Living with Fear* (Marks, 1978).

Concurrent with the education of the patient, the psychotherapist can assess the degree of the patient's disability in daily living. This will help to establish a baseline of avoidance behaviors and make it possible to monitor progress throughout treatment. Several questionnaires can aid in determining the degree of debilitation and the optimal procedures for starting treatment. For example, the Agoraphobic Cognitions Questionnaire includes items pertaining to catastrophic thoughts about the results of panic, and the Body Sensations Questionnaire asks about physical sensations associated with anxiety (Chambless et al., 1984). The Mobility Inventory provides an index of fear of travel (Chambless et al., 1985). Finally, the Fear Questionnaire (FQ) is a brief, 23-item scale for assessing social phobia or agoraphobia (Marks & Matthews, 1979). We have included copies of these measures in the Appendices section (pp. 61-74). Simple behavioral diaries can supplement the various questionnaires by having patients identify apparent precipitants to their panic attack. Of course all of these assessment tools can be readministered to assess progress in therapy.

Behavioral Models. In our view, behavioral treatment programs using graduated exposure procedures have been most successful with panic disorder patients. Other treatment programs using indirect exposure (systematic desensitization, imaginal flooding), cognitive modification, or strictly verbal psychotherapies have a much lower

31

success rate. Of course, indirect exposure and cognitive modification procedures can be added to enhance the effectiveness of direct exposure.

Several authors have described the direct exposure methods in detail (Barlow & Waddell, 1985; Beck & Emery, 1985; Weekes, 1984; Zane & Milt, 1984). These programs all require exposure to the feared panic attacks. Patients can substantially reduce or eliminate panic attacks when they learn to identify their precursors through monitoring their thoughts and mental images. Outcome studies have shown that about 70% of the patients with graduated exposure programs show clinically significant improvement.

Behavioral treatment programs are commonly combined with adjunctive treatments such as spousal involvement or paradoxical intention. Spouses can aid therapy by becoming more knowledgeable about the phobic and by accompanying the patient on outings. Involving the spouse may also strengthen the marriage. Paradoxical intention is also useful for controlling the heightened sense of anticipatory anxiety and should be explained honestly and openly without any effort to trick the patient.

Often when the graduated exposure is successful, patients still feel some residual anxiety similar to a mild generalized anxiety disorder state. They do not report panic attacks but still feel high physiological arousal. In these situations, psychotherapists need to determine the origin of the "background" anxiety. In some situations, anticipatory anxiety or fear of another panic attack may cause this anxiety. In other situations it may be due to a generalized worry about life situations in general.

If fear of future panic attacks causes the background anxiety, then psychotherapists need to determine if the patient continues to have minor or monosymptomatic panic attacks. If so, more work needs to be done to control these attacks. If the patient is not having panic attacks but still fears them, the therapist needs to explain how the fear of the panic attacks developed over many years and will dissipate with time as the patient has more and more success in subverting the attacks and achieving mobility.

If a generalized fear of a number of situations causes the background anxiety, then the psychotherapist may need to treat the patient as a generalized anxiety disorder

(GAD) patient (see the section entitled "Generalized Anxiety Disorder," pp. 51-54). In either case, these patients may benefit from relaxation procedures, cognitive procedures to identify anxiety-invoking thoughts, or benzodiazepines to reduce the background anxiety. Finally, many patients with panic disorders have co-existing psychological problems that also need attention.

Pharmacological Approaches. Several medications are useful for the treatment of panic disorders (Sheehan, 1984). Although the exact pharmacological mechanisms are not known, the medications appear to raise the threshold for the development of panic attacks. Many patients report that medication significantly reduces or eliminates spontaneous panic attacks, although these patients may still experience panic in crisis situations. Interestingly, successful responders to medication no longer produce sodium lactate-induced panic attacks.

The pharmacotherapist has several medications from which to choose. Tricyclic antidepressants (TCAs) have proven successful in reducing panic attacks. Monamine oxidase inhibitors (MAOIs) have a slightly higher success rate but require strict dietary precautions (Sheehan, 1984). Recently, alprazolam (Xanax) also has been found to reduce panic attacks. Of the patients who complete pharmacological treatments, 50% show substantial improvement and another 30% show moderate improvement. However, the rest drop out of treatment because of their inability or unwillingness to tolerate side effects. Another 33% will refuse even to try a pharmacological treatment. Consequently, only about 50% of patients presenting for treatment of panic disorders will benefit from medications.

The pharmacotherapist needs to consider several factors in choosing between antidepressants and alprazolam to suppress panic attacks. Alprazolam works faster in controlling panic attacks, but does not have as much effect on depression as the other drugs. The discontinuation of alprazolam almost always leads to a sudden recurrence of the panic attacks and to withdrawal symptoms. Antidepressants, however, have a lower rate of relapse. Goldstein (1986) suggested maximizing the positive qualities of both medications by starting the patient on alprazolam to suppress panic attacks rapidly, and then gradually switching to antidepressants which have a more broad-based positive impact. Patients who fail to respond to the tricyclic antidepressants can be switched to MAOIs, which are generally more potent in addressing symptoms than the TCAs.

According to Sheehan (1984), the use of medications to suppress panic attacks does not eliminate the need for behavior therapy. Rather, Sheehan follows a two-step procedure in which the medication reduces the panic attacks followed by behavior therapy (through desensitization or graduated exposure) to reduce the phobic avoidance.

A CASE VIGNETTE

Marvin is a 36-year-old unemployed laborer referred to a mental health clinic by his family doctor. He complained of attacks of numbness in his arms, dizziness, and buzzing in his ears. He had not experienced any of these attacks in the last month, but he was afraid they would occur again. He described anticipatory anxiety at work and nervousness around people in general. He reported being shy as a child and he apparently showed separation anxiety when he started school. A family doctor had prescribed Centrax three times a day, but Marvin complained that it did not stop his "fits." The panic attacks started when he separated from his wife 4 years ago, and he had not held steady employment since then. He said that he was afraid to return to work until he "got his strength back." The Life History Questionnaire showed a long pattern of isolation and extreme dependency upon his ex-wife and parents. Immediate family members were his only consistent source of social contact. He often drank alcohol to the point of intoxication. When drinking, he lost his social inhibitions and occasionally tried to develop a relationship with a woman at a bar. He had few friends, lived with his parents, and frequently talked about how much he missed his ex-wife. He felt nervous in shopping malls or other public places even when accompanied by his mother or other family members.

Diagnosis and Treatment Recommendations

Diagnosis. Axis I: Panic Disorder Without Agoraphobia
Axis II: Avoidant Personality Disorder

Treatment Plan. This case has all the markings of
panic disorder with agoraphobia, but it does not meet that
criterion technically because the panic attacks have not
occurred in the last month. From a treatment point of
view, however, Marvin can be considered to have a panic
disorder.

The psychotherapist needs to assess several more of
Marvin's characteristics, especially those related to a
likely longstanding avoidant personality disorder.
Although not mentioned in the vignette, Marvin is probably highly vulnerable to depression, which should be
revealed by the BDI source. Further assessment should
clarify the nature of the patient's cognitive, physiological,
and social skills functioning, since these areas are
generally problematic in social phobia.

Other possible starting points for treatment depend on
the results of further assessment. Social skills training
most likely would be indicated for a patient manifesting
avoidant personality disorder. The treatment of his panic
disorder would be the same as for any panic disorder
patient.

Therapists may find several self-report measures to be
helpful in understanding the patient's anxiety disorder.
Several inventories are reproduced in the Appendices
section.

OBSESSIVE-COMPULSIVE DISORDERS

Robert is a 24-year-old married postal employee.
He comes from a strict religious family and is an
active member in his local church. He recently
became the father of a healthy baby girl. For the
past several months he has been bothered by
intrusive thoughts and images of harming his wife
and baby. He has had clear mental pictures of
strangling his wife and throwing their baby into
their wood burning stove. These images have
created a great deal of anxiety, but he has not

been able to stop them. He has never acted violent-
ly toward anyone and appears to be an active and
loving father.

Robert has an obsessive-compulsive disorder (OCD).
The *DSM-III-R* defines obsessions as "persistent ideas,
thoughts, impulses, or images that are experienced, at
least initially, as intrusive and senseless" (p. 245). The
DSM-III-R defines compulsions as

> repetitive, purposeful, and intentional behaviors
> that are performed in response to an obsession, ac-
> cording to certain rules, or in a stereotyped
> fashion. The behavior is designed to neutralize or
> prevent discomfort or some dreaded event or
> situation. However, either the activity is not con-
> nected in a realistic way with what it is designed
> to neutralize or prevent, or it is clearly excessive.
> The act is performed with a sense of subjective
> compulsion coupled with a desire to resist that
> compulsion (at least initially). (p. 245)

The OCD disorders appear with equal frequency in
men and women. These disorders have a bimodal age of
onset and commonly appear in early adolescence or in the
late 20s. Onset often follows a major life event such as
the birth of a child, start of a new job, or moving to a
different place. Onset beyond the age of 35 is rare and,
in such cases, a neurological evaluation is advisable to
rule out possible organic causes. Medical and neurological
evaluations when the onset is before the age of 35 are
almost always negative (Jenike, 1983).

DIFFERENTIAL DIAGNOSIS

Obsessions and compulsions often occur in other
diagnostic categories of the *DSM-III-R*, and it is important to distinguish the OCD from other major disorders.
Sometimes the line between obsessions and schizophrenia
is hard to draw, but one distinction is that most schizo-
phrenics view their unusual thoughts and impulses as ego-
syntonic. That is, the schizophrenic considers them
realistic and reasonable, whereas OCD patients find the
obsessions and compulsions ego-dystonic. This distinction
is helpful most of the time, although it is sometimes diffi-

cult to distinguish an overvalued idea of an OCD patient from a delusion. (See discussion below.)

Compulsions or stereotypic movements sometimes occur in organic brain syndrome (OBS) patients or in those having Tourette's syndrome. In OBS patients the repetitive behaviors are caused by an inability to vary performances and are not anxiety reducing behaviors. In Tourette's syndrome the symptoms are generated by a neurological condition, serve no purpose, and do not reduce anxiety.

The distinction between depression and obsessions may also be difficult to establish. At times obsessions result from depression and disappear as the depression is treated, and at other times the depression results from or follows the OCD. The rule is to look for the sequence of symptom development. Depression following the onset of the OCD may be more properly characterized as demoralization. The OCD symptoms alone are likely to lead to feelings of despair, hopelessness, and self-reproach. In fact, both Turner, McCann, et al. (1986) and Barlow et al. (1986) found the average OCD patient to have Beck Depression Inventory scores high enough to qualify as major depression (see Table 3, p. 7), but these symptoms do not necessarily warrant a diagnosis of depression. Vegetative symptoms of depression most commonly distinguish primary depression from demoralization. For patients with vegetative symptoms or a depression which was present before the OCD, it is necessary to treat the depression first either with psychotherapy or with medication before working on the obsessions and compulsions (Steketee & Foa, 1985).

A distinction needs to be made between OCD and compulsive personality disorder. Persons having compulsive personality disorders show a pre-occupation with details that have a ritualistic quality, but the compulsions are ego-syntonic and have no anxiety reducing features. Many OCD patients have compulsive traits, and about half of them have pre-morbid personalities with compulsive traits (Jenike, 1983).

The risk of having OCD plus an associated anxiety disorder is also high. Many OCD patients report simple or social phobias, panic disorders, agoraphobia, or motor tics.

Finally, a small proportion of OCD patients have schizotypal personality disorders (Jenike, Baer, & Minichiello, 1987): They frequently display odd speech, suspiciousness, and hypersensitivity; they have inadequate social support systems and are socially isolated; and they are characterized by magical thinking, ideas of reference, and depersonalization. Unless the schizotypal features are addressed, these patients will respond poorly to standard treatments for OCD.

SUBTYPES OF OBSESSIVE-COMPULSIVE DISORDERS

The different subtypes of obsessive-compulsive disorders require different kinds of treatment. The most common subtype presents obsessions followed by compulsions, such as a compulsion to clean or to avoid contamination from dirt or other noxious substances. Another OCD subtype includes those who experience obsessions without compulsions. This subgroup often describes obsessions with violating important social norms such as acting aggressively or sexually. A final rare form of OCD is called primary obsessional slowness. Patients with this condition act as though life were in slow motion and take many hours to perform simple routine life skills such as shaving, washing, or dressing.

Psychotherapists may find the Maudsley Obsessional-Compulsive Inventory (MOC) (Hodgson & Rachman, 1977) helpful in assessing the existence and extent of different obsessive-compulsive complaints. This inventory yields information about observable rituals of cleaning, checking, slowness, and doubting. The inventory is quick (10-15 minutes) and easy to administer (30 items in a true-false format), controls for an acquiescent response set, and includes only items that differentiate obsessional from nonobsessional neurotics. A copy of the MOC is reprinted in the Appendices section (pp. 73-74). A total score and subscale scores for cleaning, checking, slowness, and doubtings are obtained by totaling the number of questions that are answered in the obsessional direction. Table 5 (p. 39) compares mean number of responses on the MOC by obsessionals and by nonobsessional neurotics.

TREATMENTS FOR OBSESSIVE-COMPULSIVE DISORDERS

For many years the treatment of OCD was difficult and characterized by low success rates. Even these modest success rates were artificially elevated because the earlier studies often included compulsive personality disorders within the category of OCD. Now advances in

TABLE 5: DATA FOR OBSESSIONAL AND NON-OBSESSIONAL NEUROTIC INDIVIDUALS*

| | Obsessionals (N = 100) | | Neurotics (N = 50) | |
	Mean	Standard Deviation	Mean	Standard Deviation
Total	18.86	4.92	9.27	5.43
Checking	6.10	2.21	2.84	2.29
Cleaning	5.55	3.04	2.38	1.97
Slowness	3.63	1.93	2.27	1.09
Doubting	5.39	1.60	3.69	1.99

*Note: From "Obsessional Compulsive Complaints" by R. J. Hodgson and S. Rachman, 1977, Behaviour Research and Therapy, 15, pp. 389-395. Copyright © 1977 by the Pergamon Journals, Ltd. Reprinted with permission.

behavioral and pharmacological treatments have led to new hope for these patients.

Obsessions with Compulsions. The optimal treatments for OCD vary according to the subtype of the disorder and the presence of co-existing disorders. Response prevention is the optimal treatment for obsessions followed by compulsions. Typically these patients have cleaning compulsions (and obsessions of dirt or filth) or checking compulsions (and obsessional doubt or guilt). Briefly, response prevention means exposing the patient for prolonged periods (45 minutes to 2 hours) to situations that produce anxiety. Often the anxiety can be heightened by having the patient engage in the most feared activities, for example, touching a "contaminated" object. In the past these patients would use avoidance or rituals, such as cleaning dirt or checking stoves, to reduce their anxiety. In response prevention, however, they are not permitted to engage in these anxiety reducing rituals. Instead, they are exposed to the very stimuli that upset them the most. They stay in the situation until their anxiety dissipates, and the exposure is graded so that mildly upsetting situations will precede the most upsetting ones. Leaving the situation before the anxiety decreases is counter-therapeutic and strengthens rather than weakens the relationship between anxiety and avoidance. Often the patient needs 10 to 20 sessions before treatment is completed (Steketee & Foa, 1985).

Outcome studies in a variety of treatment centers have found success rates with response prevention of about 75% for patients who comply with treatment (Steketee & Foa, 1985). Follow-up studies show that the treatment effects last, although some patients may require booster sessions. The outcome for response prevention is substantially higher than for any other treatment program for obsessive-compulsive disorders (Steketee & Foa, 1985). As noted previously, if severe depression co-exists with the OCD, then medication or psychotherapy for the depression is indicated before beginning the response prevention program.

Response prevention has not been so successful with a minority of obsessive-compulsives who have "overvalued ideas." These patients adhere with rigidity to certain illogical ideas, assigning high probabilities to feared consequences. Patients, for example, may insist that they have AIDS and seek repeated blood tests that all prove negative. Such persistent beliefs complicate treatment and usually must be altered before significant improvement can be made (Steketee & Foa, 1985).

If the patients' failures with fixed ideas were deleted from the outcome studies, then the success rate with response prevention for OCD exceeds the 75% figure cited by Steketee and Foa (1985). The distinction between schizophrenic delusions and obsessional, overvalued ideas may be difficult to make. Although typical schizophrenic and obsessive thought patterns are usually distinct, overvalued ideas represent a gray area in which the distinction between the two becomes blurred. In OCD these overvalued ideas may impede therapy, but psychotic decompensation is rare. The assessment of obsessives with compulsive rituals should include a clear distinction between obsessions and compulsions, and between active and passive avoidance. This dichotomy of obsessions and compulsions suggested by Steketee and Foa (1985) is helpful in the design of response prevention programs. Assessment of OCD requires identifying the obsessions (anxiety inducing thoughts or acts) and compulsions (anxiety reducing thoughts or acts). For response prevention to succeed the anxiety reducing compulsions must be blocked, which requires identifying the compulsions, even cognitive ones. Usually behavioral compulsions are easily identifiable because they are overt behavioral acts. However, cognitive compulsions such as repeating a prayer, mantra, or a ritualistic saying will be more difficult to identify. The patient must block these cognitive compulsions through distraction or thought stopping in order for response prevention to have its maximum success.

In addition, the psychotherapist needs to identify active and passive forms of avoidance. Active avoidance is easily recognized, as in the compulsive who cleans incessantly. Passive avoidance is more difficult to detect. Examples include persons who sit at the edge of the chair to avoid becoming soiled, who open doors with the tips of their fingers to avoid being contaminated, or avoid going places they associate with disease or germs. A successful response prevention program must overcome both passive avoidance as well as the more obvious active avoidance patterns.

Obsessions without Compulsions. Obsessives without compulsions are harder to treat. The psychotherapist has several treatment options from which to choose, each with lower rates of success (about 50% or less) than response prevention treatment of obsessions with compulsions. The treatment techniques we recommend include paradoxical techniques, operant conditioning, or assertiveness training. The latter may be applicable when obsessions are of hurting other people, and it is assumed that aggression/assertiveness issues predominate.

Tricyclic antidepressants (TCAs) also have demonstrated some success with this group. A number of case reports have cited dramatic improvements in response to TCAs. The responses, however, were not predictable or linked to previous levels of depression, and treatment failures are common (Jenike, 1983). When these medications work, they appear to have some antiobsessional qualities distinct from their antidepressant effects. One antidepressant, Clomipramine, has been effective with OCD, but it is available in the United States only at research sites sponsored by the National Institute of

Mental Health. Like TCAs, monoamine oxidase inhibitors have had occasional dramatic success.

No outcome study has yet directly compared TCAs with the various behavior therapy techniques in a group of obsessional patients. We suggest starting treatment with the nondepressed obsessional patient with either the behavioral or TCA approach, but remaining flexible enough to consider adjunctive treatments or to switch treatments if desired results are not forthcoming. Depressed obsessional patients should probably start with antidepressants. However, it is important to remember that demoralization is distinct from primary depression. Other pharmacological treatments such as anxiolytic agents or neuroleptics have had little success with OCD disorders.

Primary Obsessional Slowness. A small minority of OCD patients are characterized by primary obsessional slowness. Such patients take hours to perform routine tasks such as brushing teeth, shaving, or dressing. These patients differ from other OCD patients in that they have little or no anxiety. The degree of impairment can be severe and interfere with holding a job or sustaining a marriage. Several case studies show that prompting, shaping, and pacing will help this group (see e.g., Rachman, 1974).

A CASE VIGNETTE

Linda is a 36-year-old housewife whose house is immaculate. The sight of dirt being tracked into her house was enough to precipitate extreme anxiety and hours of furtive cleaning. She made her husband take showers in the basement and insisted that her children repeatedly clean their rooms. Although her husband had catered to her wishes most of the time, he was tiring of her excessive pre-occupation with cleanliness. When he talked with her about becoming more relaxed about cleaning, she insisted that household dirt transmits dreaded diseases like leukemia, cancer, and Autoimmune Deficiency Syndrome (AIDS). No amount of persuasion seemed to convince her otherwise.

Diagnosis and Treatment Recommendations

Diagnosis. Axis I: Obsessive-Compulsive Disorder
            Axis II: No Information

Treatment Plan. Acquiring Linda's cooperation will be difficult because of her fixed belief that her concerns are legitimate. If she does agree to treatment, however, response prevention is recommended for obsessions followed by compulsions. Depression should be assessed through the BDI or other instruments. The presence of any significant amount of depression may suggest the use of antidepressant medication.

POST-TRAUMATIC STRESS DISORDER

Phillip is a 40-year-old Vietnam veteran who was awarded a Purple Heart. Although he is proud of his military service in Vietnam, he seldom talks about it. For the previous 3 months he has had nightmares about an incident involving the death of several Vietnamese children. He had never discussed this event with anyone since he separated from the military and appeared to have forgotten it completely. He has become increasingly irritable and emotionally distant from his wife, and vegetative symptoms of depression have emerged. He mentioned his nightmares after several sessions of therapy and after reading an article about Post-Traumatic Stress Disorder (PTSD). The nightmares started shortly after a car struck and injured his youngest son.

Phillip has post-traumatic stress disorder (PTSD). Although recent research has focused on emotionally disturbed Vietnam veterans, there is growing recognition that many types of catastrophes such as rape, crime victimization, torture, floods, or other natural catastrophes can cause PTSD. The essential feature of PTSD is that the syndrome develops out of a trauma (like Phillip's combat experience) which is "out of the range of normal human experience" (*DSM-III-R*, p. 248).

The characteristic symptoms include (a) persistent re-experiencing of the traumatic event through recurrent and intrusive recollections, dreams, and/or flashbacks, and intense distress at exposure to events that symbolize

43

or resemble the original trauma; (b) persistent avoidance of stimuli related to the trauma through numbing of responsiveness; and (c) increased arousal resulting in symptoms such as difficulty sleeping, outbursts of anger, exaggerated startle response, and hypervigilance (*DSM-III-R*).

The PTSD can have either an acute or delayed onset. Acute PTSD occurs immediately or soon after the trauma. Delayed symptoms may first appear several months or even years after the trauma. The delayed-onset phenomenon is well-documented, although less frequent than acute PTSD. Usually triggering events remind these patients of their vulnerability to loss and trauma.

Reliable information on the prevalence, duration, sex ratio, and natural course of the disorder is lacking. Although anecdotal information is extensive, scientific research on PTSD is more limited. Anecdotal reports from a variety of sources such as combat fatigued American soldiers in World War II, histories of survivors of natural catastrophes such as floods, accounts of survivors of assaults and rape, and documentations of the experiences of concentration camp survivors and survivors of Hiroshima all give evidence of anxiety disorders that meet the PTSD criteria of the *DSM-III-R*. Although greatly valued, these anecdotal histories do not contain information on the course of the disorder, and they lack standardized psychometric data and uniform interviewing procedures.

The anecdotal evidence, however, suggests that the disorder can fluctuate over time and become worse in the presence of triggering stimuli or at the anniversary of the original trauma. For example, warm, humid weather may trigger a flashback in a survivor of a Japanese POW camp, or the odor of a certain male antiperspirant deodorant may evoke a PTSD response in a survivor of a rape or assault.

Reliable information about the incidence of the PTSD in the general population is lacking. Studies of war veterans report that PTSD can be found in 5% to 25% of active duty soldiers, army reservists, and veterans. No precise data are available of PTSD in other survivor groups, although it is frequently found among survivors of concentration camps (Krystal, 1968), violent crimes (Bard & Sangry, 1986), natural catastrophes (Raphael, 1986), and tortured political prisoners (Somnier & Genefke, 1986). No information is available on sex ratios, and the age of onset varies according to the survivor's age at the time of the trauma.

The PTSD can also occur in persons such as military nurses or rescue workers who are exposed to the carnage of the war or catastrophe. Usually the likelihood of developing PTSD increases when there is exposure to human mutilation or corpses. Military medics and nurses exposed to the carnage are especially vulnerable to developing PTSD (Van Devanter & Morgan, 1984).

DIFFERENTIAL DIAGNOSIS

The *DSM-III* provided a major advance in formally recognizing the sufferings of trauma survivors, which previously had been underestimated. The *DSM-I* had a diagnostic category called "gross stress reaction," but it specified that this reaction would dissipate quickly. The *DSM-II* also included a category for short-lived, trauma-induced symptoms called "transient situational disturbance." These previous diagnostic categories minimized the effects of the trauma and emphasized the pre-existing difficulties of the individual. The category of PTSD first appeared in the *DSM-III*. The *DSM-III-R* diagnosis of PTSD requires that the triggering event be so stressful as to create a disturbance in virtually everyone. Although the form of trauma will vary, PTSD survivors are similar enough that generalizations may be made regardless of the nature of the trauma.

The research and clinical literatures suggest that the numbing/intrusiveness dimension is the essential feature of PTSD. After periods of extreme stress, a person may block out or deny certain experiences. Concentration camp survivors, rape victims, torture survivors, and combat veterans often avoid talking about their experiences or talk only about the experiences least upsetting for them. Combat veterans, for example, may tell war stories in a casual manner. This may be misleading and give the impression that the war was not particularly bothersome for them. In fact, many veterans talk around their upsetting experiences and refuse to mention their severe traumas and losses.

This denial can be so thorough that friends, relatives, and even some unsuspecting psychotherapists do not recognize PTSD symptoms. This happened when American and German psychiatrists interviewed concentration camp survivors following World War II in order to evaluate their eligibility to receive disability benefits. These interviews initially declared many survivors to be normal and free of psychiatric disability. The survivors themselves usually denied any severe psychiatric problems, or else greatly minimized them.

Similar experiences were found in the evaluation of the survivors of the Buffalo Creek flood in West Virginia (Krystal, 1968). The survivors of the Buffalo Creek flood had instituted a multimillion dollar lawsuit against the owners of the dam which broke and flooded the valley. As part of the lawsuit, legal counsel had hired mental health experts to assess the degree of psychological impairment. Although the plaintiffs had financial incentives to exaggerate their symptoms, they did not. On the contrary, the majority minimized or denied them (Titchener & Kapp, 1976).

The second component of the numbing dimension is the presence of intrusive thoughts. This feature may take the form of nightmares, déjà vu experiences, or memories triggered by relatively innocuous pictures or events. Some survivors have been mistakenly identified as schizophrenic because of the strength of the intrusive memories. A woman walking down the streets of New York had a sudden feeling that she was back in the concentration camps. This experience, however, was not an hallucination as found within schizophrenia, but an intrusive thought or memory caused by a triggering object in the environment (Krystal, 1968). At times survivors re-enact elements of the traumatic event. Re-enactments by combat veterans may take the form of aggressive behavior, and assaults on innocent bystanders have been reported.

Research with combat veterans suggests that the two predominant symptoms, re-experiencing and denial, tend to be divided according to the nature of precipitating events. Veterans who only witnessed combat tend to have re-experiencing symptoms, whereas those who participated in combat tend to show denial. The research is insufficient to determine if this distinction applies to all forms of trauma.

Generally speaking, the likelihood of developing PTSD varies directly with the severity of the event. Persons who have survived floods and fires, for example, are more likely to develop PTSD if they also lost a loved one or sustained heavy property loss. Similarly, American prisoners of war from World War II were less likely to develop psychiatric disorders if they had been imprisoned in German prison camps as opposed to Japanese prison camps, which as a whole were more traumatizing due to a higher frequency of beatings, torture, forced labor, and starvation (Beebe, 1975). The severity of the loss may depend on subtle factors. Losing family heirlooms, cherished trinkets, or photographs in a fire may, for example, be more stressful than the loss of many thousands of dollars. The threatened loss of a loved one may also be sufficient to elicit PTSD.

When traumatic experiences include ego-dystonic elements, they are especially likely to trigger PTSD. The survivors may feel guilty or ashamed of what they had done or failed to do. For example, concentration camp survivors have felt guilty because they believed they did not resist strenuously enough. Combat veterans have been overwhelmed by having had to violate their own moral codes against killing, and rape victims may doubt their innocence if they believe they did not resist their attacker aggressively enough. Survivors of torture who reveal information under duress may doubt their courage or honor. Self-attributions of guilt in survivors of trauma are frequent, and this factor may interact with their usual tendency to be too self-punitive. Women who are physically injured in the course of a rape, for example, are less likely to develop PTSD than those who are only threatened with assault. It appears that the physical injury reduces the self-doubt about their desire to resist.

Several researchers have attempted to develop more precise assessment tools for combat-related PTSD. One of the most frequently cited assessment tools is the PTSD subscale of the MMPI, developed by Keane, Malloy, and Fairbanks (1984). This scale, and others designed to assist in diagnosing PTSD, should still be regarded as a research tool or as an aide rather than a substitute for a detailed clinical interview (Vanderploeg, Sison, & Hickling, 1987). A good review of this promising area of research may be found in a special section of the *Journal of Clinical Psychology* (January 1987, Volume 43).

CO-EXISTING OR COMPLICATING DISORDERS

Often survivors of trauma have symptoms that warrant other concurrent diagnoses. To date, it is not clear whether the common co-existing diagnoses vary as a consequence of the demographic or personality features of the survivor or the nature of the trauma. Rape survivors and survivors of natural catastrophes often have co-existing major depression. It may be beneficial to inquire about the possibility of previous trauma through assault, natural catastrophe, or military experience of patients presenting mixtures of anxiety, depression, or somatic pre-occupation. Vietnam era combat veterans have a high rate of co-existing depression, drug abuse, and antisocial personality disorder. In contrast, survivors of natural disasters, torture, concentration camps, and criminal assaults usually have depression as a co-existing disorder and are less likely to demonstrate drug abuse or personality disorders. Because the majority of American Vietnam veterans came from the middle to lower classes, it is not known if their background predisposed them toward antisocial personality disorder, if men with a predisposition to develop personality disorders were more likely to seek out combat experiences, or if the combat experiences led to the development of personality disorder symptoms.

TREATMENTS FOR PTSD

PTSD is unique among psychiatric disorders and especially among anxiety disorders because there are no controlled treatment outcome studies. Existing treatment studies have all been uncontrolled or limited to case studies, and drop-out rates have often been high. Although there have been controlled studies with survivors of rape, the authors did not demonstrate that all participants had PTSD. Instead, the treatment groups were likely to have been "contaminated" with persons having other diagnoses. In part this is because the diagnosis is relatively new, appearing first in the *DSM-III*. More importantly, PTSD survivors are reluctant to participate in treatment programs, let alone outcome studies, because they characteristically minimize or deny their problems.

Several helpful case histories and uncontrolled studies, however, deal with this disorder. The treatments have followed many different theoretical orientations including psychodynamic, behavioral, and biochemical. Despite the differences in these approaches, all successful treatments re-expose the survivor to some aspect of the trauma (Fairbanks & Nicholson, 1987). This may require discussing an event that evokes high anxiety and fear, and such a painful process must be guided carefully, with an effort to reduce the discomfort.

Recent reports suggest that group psychotherapy is a popular and appealing method for the treatment of PTSD patients. One of the benefits of group treatment is that group members can create an atmosphere of support and trust rather than the condemnation feared by many survivors. Vietnam veterans are highly sensitive to being censured for their participation in a war that lacked uniform popular support, and rape victims fear that other people will condemn them for failing to take safety precautions or to fight back hard enough.

In addition to group psychotherapy, individual behavioral approaches such as guided imagery, flooding, or variations of systematic desensitization can reduce the anxiety associated with certain triggering stimuli or thoughts. It is important to obtain the cooperation of the patient by explaining the procedures and their rationale thoroughly. Memories of the traumatic events are often so painful that patients will avoid confrontive treatments.

Cognitive restructuring of attributions is almost always indicated. As discussed previously, patients having PTSD often feel extreme survivor guilt. One of the most important functions of self-help groups is that they let survivors know what others have experienced, thereby realizing that their own reactions and behaviors were normal or understandable given the circumstances.

Severe forms of PTSD may be characterized by social withdrawal to the point of schizoid-like behavior. Although some patients regain social skills after the symptoms of PTSD are addressed, others may still need social skills training. Education of the family and friends about the nature of PTSD is almost always indicated.

Recent reports suggest that medications have benefit for some PTSD patients. The rule is to use the medication to treat the symptoms. Severe flashbacks may be treated with neuroleptics, vegetative symptoms of depression with antidepressants, and general anxiety with benzodiazepines. Imipramine has become especially popular in the treatment of PTSD, although this and other medications must be used as adjunctives to psychotherapy.

A CASE VIGNETTE

Carol, a 27-year-old single woman with a major complaint of anxiety, sought assistance from a mental health center. She insisted on talking with a female therapist. In the first interview she described a suicide attempt that took place during the past year. She reported experiencing sudden mood changes and excessive nervousness for no apparent reason. She had a poor appetite, a low level of energy, and she slept poorly at night. She had broken up with her boyfriend during the past year. Although she blamed him for the failure of the relationship, it appeared, from her description, that she had become hostile and uncompromising with him. Although her behavior had a hostile, suspicious, and almost paranoid quality, she could not stand to be alone, and she frequently sought out the company of others to avoid the anxiety she felt when alone. During the second interview the psychotherapist learned that Carol had been raped about 1 year earlier. Her functioning before that time had been good. After the rape she developed a startle response to environmental cues that reminded her of the rape experience.

She became afraid to be alone. Sex began to disgust her, and she terminated her relationship with her boyfriend (against his wishes). The very topic of rape upset her tremendously, and she seldom mentioned the experience to anyone. She blamed herself for not struggling more with her assailant. Her sleep was interrupted by frightening dreams to the point that she was afraid to go to sleep.

Diagnosis and Treatment Recommendations

Diagnosis. Axis I: PTSD
Major Depression
Axis II: No Diagnosis

Treatment Plan. The treatment should be implemented slowly and done with care not to frighten her. Given her past experience, it is reasonable to respect her preference for a female psychotherapist. Antidepressants may help relieve the depressive symptoms. Gradually the psychotherapist and patient may be able to identify cues to her startle response and institute systematic desensitization or related strategies. Eventually, the successful treatment program will allow her to talk about her experience for the first time. Eliciting the help of family members may be indicated.

GENERALIZED ANXIETY DISORDER

Thomas is a 25-year-old married mechanic who experiences persistent worry about a variety of situations. Sometimes at work he worries that he has left the gas stove turned on in his house. He worries about his wife commuting to work, and about the babysitter's ability to care for their child. He often has shaky hands and a dry mouth; he also has trouble sleeping. When he developed severe heartburn, his physician prescribed a low dosage of Ativan, a benzodiazepine.

Tom has a generalized anxiety disorder (GAD), a generalized and persistent anxiety without any of the characteristics of other anxiety disorders. That is, he does not experience sudden anxiety in the presence of a feared object, nor does he have obsessions or compulsions, panic attacks, or the intrusiveness/denial pattern found in PTSD. GAD is a residual diagnostic category to be used when other categories of anxiety disorders have been excluded.

DSM-III-R defines GAD in part as "unrealistic or excessive anxiety and worry (apprehensive expectation) about two or more life circumstances . . . for six months or longer, during which the person has been bothered by these concerns more days than not" (p. 251). The symptoms of GAD include (a) motor tension such as trembling and restlessness, (b) automatic hyperactivity characterized by symptoms such as shortness of breath, sweating, dry mouth, nausea, and so on, and (c) vigilance and scanning. The *DSM-III-R* states that at least 6 of 18 symptoms are often present. GAD may start at any age but usually begins in the 20s and 30s. The sex distribution is about equal (Thyer, Parrish, et al., 1985). Although it is psychologically taxing, GAD generally does not show the degree of impairment common to other anxiety disorders.

DIFFERENTIAL DIAGNOSIS

Because GAD is defined as a residual category, relatively few patients receive this diagnosis. At the Center for Stress and Anxiety Disorders in Albany, New York, only about 11% of the patients receive a primary diagnosis of GAD (Barlow et al., 1986). This rate corresponds roughly to findings at other anxiety disorder centers.

In some respects almost all anxiety disorder patients could receive GAD as a diagnosis because most anxious patients experience some of the GAD symptoms. The only exception is patients having simple phobias, 40% of whom could meet the criteria for GAD.

The *DSM-III-R* distinguishes between the kind of anxiety found in GAD from the anticipatory anxiety found in other anxiety disorders, especially panic disorders, based on the content of the patient's worry. Panic disorder patients frequently fear the onset of the next panic attack (anticipatory anxiety), while GAD patients express anxiety about multiple life circumstances.

The GAD differs from panic disorders in other ways as well. Although GAD patients sometimes have panic attacks, they are not frequent and do not lead to territorial apprehensiveness. Also, GAD patients experience fewer autonomic symptoms, and the onset of the disorder is earlier and more gradual than the onset of panic disorder. Furthermore, relatives of panic disorder patients have a higher than average incidence of panic disorder, but there is no such increase in the incidence of GAD among family members. To date, convincing evidence for a biological etiology of GAD is lacking (Marks, 1987). Finally, although the course of GAD tends to be chronic and unfluctuating, it appears to be easier to treat than panic disorders.

TREATMENTS FOR GAD

Because GAD is a relatively new classification which appeared first in the *DSM-III*, there are few outcome studies on it. Nevertheless, many studies done prior to the *DSM-III* appear to have used patients who could have been diagnosed as suffering from GAD, and this research suggests GAD responds well to a number of interventions. Relaxation-based treatments such as anxiety management training, applied relaxation, relaxation as self-control, or self-control desensitization can help reduce general anxiety (Barrios & Shigetomi, 1979). It is difficult to select one of these interventions rather than another because they all help the individual develop relaxation as a self-control skill that can be applied to a wide range of situations. Systematic desensitization, which is only applied in a classical conditioning format, does not appear applicable to GAD unless there is a co-existing simple or social phobia. Cognitive procedures such as outlined by Beck and Emery (1985) and Ellis (Whalen et al., 1980) also appear to be helpful for GAD problems by modifying the dysfunctional thoughts that characterize the disorder.

Benzodiazepines seem to reduce symptoms of autonomic disturbances and have few interactions and side effects (occasional drowsiness). Opinions vary regarding the abuse of and possible addiction to benzodiazepines. Whereas some believe that benzodiazepines are widely abused and therefore long-term use is not indicated, others believe that long-term use of low level dosages does not necessarily lead to dependency or addiction. Perhaps the greatest abuse of benzodiazepines would be to prescribe them without also offering psychotherapy directed at altering stressful life situations.

Persons with a history of drug and alcohol abuse are highly vulnerable to abuse of benzodiazepines, in which case a low dose of neuroleptics or antidepressants with incidental anxiety reducing features could be recommended. Despite disputes concerning the long-term use of benzodiazepines, there is little controversy that short-term low dose use can help GAD patients.

A CASE VIGNETTE

Donna is a 48-year-old lawyer with a prestigious law firm. She has a reputation for being meticulous and for researching her cases thoroughly. Some of her clients requested another lawyer because she took so long to prepare their cases. Occasionally her extreme meticulousness paid off, and she found an unusual legal precedent or theory which made a difference in court. She would usually develop somatic anxiety while worrying about details of case preparation. Donna was not satisfied with her performance and continually worried about doing the best job she could. She had trouble sleeping at nights, and often returned to work late at night to check and double check the references and style of writing in her briefs. Her worries were not confined to work. She often ruminated unnecessarily about her children's health or family finances.

Diagnosis and Treatment Recommendations

Diagnosis. Axis I: Generalized Anxiety Disorder
Axis II: Insufficient Information

Treatment Plan. Donna demonstrates anxiety that has generalized to a wide range of situations. She shows some signs of compulsivity in that her perfectionism at work interferes with job performance. At this point it is not clear whether the perfectionism is an enduring trait or a consequence of anxiety about job performance. Although Donna did report some vegetative symptoms of anxiety, she emphasized vigilance and apprehensive expectation. On the basis of this information, a cognitive approach appears indicated.

CHILDREN'S ANXIETY DISORDERS

Sally is a third grader who refuses to go to school. At first she complained that she was sick. Although the pediatrician accepted her vague symptoms as legitimate at first, it eventually became clear that there was nothing physically wrong with her. At times her mother has tried to make her go to school, but Sally cries, fights, and rebels until her mother lets her stay home. Sally's refusal is a mystery to her teacher, who had found her to be well-behaved, polite, and above-average in school performance.

The *DSM-III-R* lists several different anxiety disorders unique to children: separation anxiety disorder, overanxious disorder, and avoidant disorders of childhood or adolescence. We provide special attention to separation anxiety disorder because overanxious disorder and avoidant disorders of childhood have near equivalents in the adult GAD and avoidant personality disorder described previously.

Of course children may experience any of the other anxiety disorders as well. Even panic disorder has been diagnosed in children, although this is rare. Children usually have simple phobias, obsessive-compulsive disorders, and post-traumatic stress disorder, and although the diagnostic criteria are the same for children as for adults, these disorders have unique features in children that have treatment implications.

54

SEPARATION ANXIETY DISORDER

The *DSM-III-R* defines separation anxiety disorder as "excessive anxiety, for at least two weeks, concerning separation from those to whom the child is attached" (p. 58). It is characterized by at least three of the following: (a) unrealistic fear of harm to parents, guardians, or loved ones; (b) unrealistic worry about calamitous events; (c) persistent reluctance or refusal to go to school or leave home; (d) refusal to go to sleep without parents nearby; (e) vague physical complaints on school days; (f) excessive distress upon separation from parents; (g) repeated nightmares concerning separation; (h) recurrent complaints of excessive distress in anticipation of separation from home and parents; or (i) fear of being away from home alone.

It is common for children to show fear of unfamiliar circumstances such as a new day care center or a new teacher. Often children will balk temporarily at having to go to school. Firm insistence and emotional support from parents is sufficient to eliminate this fear in the vast majority of children. Separation anxiety disorders should only be diagnosed when the school refusal is persistent and the other *DSM-III-R* criteria are met.

Often the separation anxiety disorder is precipitated by an illness suffered by the child, death or illness of a person in the child's home, divorce of the parents, or a change of schedule. The disorder is more common when the child changes school buildings, faces a family move, is promoted from elementary to middle school, or after long vacations or illnesses. Unfortunately the parents may inadvertently reinforce the separation anxiety by catering to the "sick" child, or exaggerating the difficulties at school.

Children with separation anxiety disorder are more likely to be female, pre-pubertal, and from lower socio-economic backgrounds. Their mothers are more likely to suffer from major depressions or anxiety disorders than mothers of other children, and one-third of separation anxiety children also can be diagnosed as having over-anxious disorder (Last et al., 1987).

Differential Diagnosis. The correct diagnosis of separation anxiety disorder requires the differentiation of the reasons for failure to attend school or leave the parents. In the past, many clinicians failed to distinguish separation anxiety from a fear (phobia) of something in school. If the child has an actual fear of something in school, then simple phobia may be the proper diagnosis. In other cases the child may have avoidant disorder of childhood (which implies a fear of strangers), may experience social anxiety, or be subjected to an unfriendly or harsh environment in school.

Separation anxiety disorder also requires a differentiation from other disorders such as major depression and conduct disorder. In major depression the symptoms of separation anxiety disorder exist along with symptoms of depression such as loss of appetite, insomnia, fatigue, and melancholia and continue even when the parents are present. Psychotherapists also need to distinguish separation anxiety disorder from conduct disorders. Some school refusals are part of a pattern in which the rights of others are chronically violated. Although conduct disorder children may refuse to go to school, they are not excessively attached to their parents and are not cooperative in other aspects of family life.

The patient having separation anxiety disorder has a good prognosis unless the condition is chronic. The optimal interventions, whether they include family therapy, behavior therapy, or others, all involve getting the child back to the school environment as soon as possible. Although the child may resist at first, failing to place the child back in school only makes treatment more difficult later, and adjustment to school is usually adequate. Because parents are likely to have difficulty insisting on school attendance, they usually need emotional support. As noted previously, many of the mothers also have depression or anxiety and may require concurrent treatment.

OVERANXIOUS DISORDER

The overanxious disorder of childhood is characterized by at least four of the following: (a) unrealistic worry about the future; (b) pre-occupation with the appropriateness of past behavior; (c) overconcern with competence in school or other tasks; (d) excessive need for reassurance; (e) physical complaints; (f) marked self-consciousness or tendency to be easily embarrassed; or (g) severe feelings of tension or inability to relax. This disorder appeared first in the *DSM-III*, and few studies or data are available. It appears to correspond roughly to that of GAD in adults. The classification from which it is most likely to require differentiation is adjustment disorder with anxious mood, in which the child has transitory symptoms precipitated by a stressful life change.

Until we learn more, treatment should follow the same pattern as GAD with adults, emphasizing cognitive reassurance and relaxation techniques modified for children (Koeppen, 1974). Parental involvement is usually needed to insure practice of relaxation exercises, to reinforce cognitive changes, and to alter parental patterns which may inadvertently exacerbate the disorder. Cognitive strategies for children may involve bibliotherapy (Sarafino, 1986) or mutual story-tellings, and parents may need to learn listening techniques so they can better understand their child's concerns.

AVOIDANT DISORDERS OF CHILDHOOD OR ADOLESCENCE

The *DSM-III-R* defines the avoidant disorder as "an excessive shrinking from contact with unfamiliar people that is of sufficient severity to interfere with social functioning in peer relationships and that is of at least six months duration" (p. 61). In addition, these children show a clear desire for social interactions with familiar people, and relationships with family members are warm and satisfying.

This disorder was also new to the *DSM-III*, and no studies or data are available. It appears to correspond roughly to avoidant personality disorder in adults and is most likely to require differentiation from separation anxiety disorder. In separation anxiety disorder the child has no fear of strangers when accompanied by parents or guardians, whereas in avoidance disorder, the child is afraid of strangers in most situations. Also, the anxiety is not pervasive, as in overanxious disorders, and is limited to contact with strangers. Because it appears to be a mild or early version of avoidant personality disorder, the psychotherapist should look for traits that characterize avoidant personality disorder, such as low self-esteem and poor social skills.

No treatment outcome studies are available yet. Nevertheless, the nature of the disorder suggests that some of the procedures used for the treatment of social phobia may be indicated: relaxation, cognitive restructuring, and social skills training. As always with children, extensive parental involvement is required, and strategies need to be modified for the child's developmental level.

CHILDHOOD EQUIVALENTS
OF ADULT DISORDERS

Children can have simple phobias, obsessive-compulsive disorders, or post-traumatic stress disorders, but panic disorders are so rare that we will not discuss them. The nature of childhood phobias varies according to the developmental stage of the child. As a rule, young children tend to fear physical harm from such sources as dogs or large animals, whereas older children fear social embarrassment in situations such as a bully's intimidation or rejection by schoolmates or teachers. In part, this differing pattern of fears occurs because the older child has different social demands like attending school and being exposed to a wider range of people than the younger child. Girls tend to report more fears than boys, although this may be due to sex role stereotypes which allow girls more latitude in expressing fear.

Transient childhood fears are very common, and psychotherapists need to differentiate simple phobias from normal fears. Normal fears tend to be more age specific, to create relatively less fear, to be amenable to normal reassurance, and to subside within 2 years without treatment.

The treatment of childhood phobias corresponds roughly to the treatment for simple phobias for adults (Johnson, 1985). As with other childhood disorders the psychotherapist must emphasize family and environmental variables that may inadvertently maintain or create the phobia. A parent who shows extreme anxiety may be modeling fear for the child, or a sibling who teases or misinforms a younger child may have induced a phobia. Parents may also contribute to creating a phobia by "protecting" the child from normal situations that would engender moderate anxiety in any child.

Systematic desensitization modified for children has been effective, but the therapist can also rely on a variety of modeling and operant conditioning procedures. Because the parents have so much control over their child's environment, well-constructed programs like this are usually successful. Of course skill acquisition techniques, such as animal management for overcoming fear of dogs, may help some children conquer their phobias.

Obsessive-compulsive disorders often start in childhood, especially in early adolescence. The treatment procedures are the same with children as with adults, and education of the parents is crucial. Parents need to understand the nature of the treatments and, if the treatment is response prevention, how these procedures may temporarily create some anxiety. Their failure to participate in the program as instructed will subvert the therapeutic effort and lead to future demoralization.

Post-traumatic stress disorder can occur at any age. Recent changes in the *DSM-III-R* recognize unique PTSD symptoms that can occur in children such as repetitive play, drawings, or dreams of the traumatic event. Diminished interest in activities and constriction of emotions are difficult for young children to report, and careful evaluation of symptoms by parents, teachers, and others is warranted.

A child's reactions to trauma used to be attributed largely to parental reactions. Although that generalization may be true for many stressful events, massive trauma can cause PTSD in children independent of parental reactions (Eth & Pynoos, 1985) and its effects may depend on the age, sex, developmental level of the child, or the nature of the trauma. Nevertheless, the research is not conclusive about the differential effects on children (Eth & Pynoos, 1985).

A CASE VIGNETTE

Shelly is a 4-year-old who is afraid to go to sleep at night. She will not even go upstairs to her room alone. The fear began a year ago after she saw a bat in her room. Shortly thereafter, her older brother began to tease her about ghosts and monsters at night. Her parents have been unable to persuade her to go to sleep by herself, and she insists on sleeping in their bedroom. Shelly becomes very upset if she is pressured to sleep alone. If they move her to her room in the middle of the night, while asleep, she will go back to her parents' room immediately when she wakens.

Diagnosis and Treatment Recommendations

Diagnosis. Axis I: Simple Phobia

Treatment Plan. Although childhood fears are common, this fear is interfering with Shelly's daily functioning, thus warranting the diagnosis of simple phobia.

Because the phobia appears to have been created by a cognitive misinterpretation of the danger of bats and monsters, we recommend a multimodal treatment that would involve cognitive restructuring, positive reinforcement, and graduated exposure. The cognitive restructuring is modified to a child's perspective and could involve reading children's books about monsters and fears (see Sarafino [1986] for recommendations of several appropriate books). The parents can play games with Shelly in which ghosts, monsters, and other imaginary creatures are mocked and treated as make-believe. Of course the older brother needs to stop telling ghost stories. Through graduated exposure, Shelly can spend more and more time upstairs alone with positive reinforcements given for "brave" behaviors.

SUMMARY

The *DSM-III-R* reflects substantial improvement in the diagnosis of anxiety disorders. A recurrent theme of this guide, however, is that the basic *DSM-III-R* label is not sufficient to select the optimal treatment. Instead, the psychotherapist may need to know the origins of the anxiety disorder, the co-existence of other disorders, or other characteristics and assets of the patients. The authors have presented research to make the treatment decisions as explicit as possible. Psychotherapists can add their clinical judgment to this empirical data in making the treatment decisions.

APPENDICES

APPENDIX A: AGORAPHOBIC
COGNITIONS QUESTIONNAIRE*

Below are some thoughts or ideas that may pass through your mind when you are nervous or frightened.

Indicate how often each thought occurs when you are nervous. Rate from 1-5 using the scale below.

1 = Thought never occurs.
2 = Thought rarely occurs.
3 = Thought occurs during half of the time I am nervous.
4 = Thought usually occurs.
5 = Thought always occurs when I am nervous.

____ I am going to throw up.

____ I am going to pass out.

____ I must have a brain tumor.

____ I will have a heart attack.

____ I will choke to death.

____ I am going to act foolish.

____ I am going blind.

____ I will not be able to control myself.

____ I will hurt someone.

____ I am going to have a stroke.

____ I am going to go crazy.

____ I am going to scream.

____ I am going to babble or talk funny.

____ I will be paralyzed by fear.

____ OTHER IDEAS NOT LISTED (Please describe and rate them)

The total score is derived by averaging all the responses. Panic disorder patients average 2.8 (SD = .8) before treatment and 2.1 (SD = .9) 6 months after treatment.

---

*Note: From "Assessment of Fear in Agoraphobia: The Body Sensations Questionnaire and the Agoraphobic Cognitions Questionnaire" by D. Chambless, G. Caputo, P. Bright, and R. Gallagher, 1984, *Journal of Consulting and Clinical Psychology*, 52, pp. 1090-1097. Copyright © 1984 by the Pergamon Journals, Ltd. Reprinted by permission.

Diagnosis and Treatment Selection for Anxiety Disorders

APPENDIX B: BODY
SENSATIONS QUESTIONNAIRE*

Below is a list of specific body sensations that may occur when you are nervous or in a feared situation. Please mark down how afraid you are of these feelings. Use a five-point scale from Not frightened to Extremely frightened.

1 = Not frightened or worried by this sensation.
2 = Somewhat frightened by this sensation.
3 = Moderately frightened by this sensation.
4 = Very frightened by this sensation.
5 = Extremely frightened by this sensation.

____ 1. Heart palpitations

____ 2. Pressure or a heavy feeling in chest

____ 3. Numbness in arms or legs

____ 4. Tingling in the fingertips

____ 5. Numbness in another part of your body

____ 6. Feeling short of breath

____ 7. Dizziness

____ 8. Blurred or distorted vision

____ 9. Nausea

____ 10. Having "butterflies" in your stomach

____ 11. Feeling a knot in your stomach

____ 12. Having a lump in your throat

____ 13. Wobbly or rubber legs

____ 14. Sweating

____ 15. A dry throat

____ 16. Feeling disoriented and confused

---

*Note: From "Assessment of Fear in Agoraphobia: The Body Sensations Questionnaire and the Agoraphobic Cognitions Questionnaire" by D. Chambless, G. Caputo, P. Bright, and R. Gallagher, 1984, Journal of Consulting and Clinical Psychology, 52, pp. 1090-1097. Copyright © 1984 by the Pergamon Journals, Ltd. Reprinted by permission.

65

____ 17. Feeling disconnected from your body: only partly present

____ 18. Other _____

Please describe _____

_____

The total score is derived by averaging responses across individual items. Panic disorder patients average 2.9 (SD = 1.3) before treatment and 1.7 (SD = 1.0) 6 months after treatment.

APPENDIX C: MOBILITY
INVENTORY FOR AGORAPHOBIA*

Name: _____ Date:_____

1. Please indicate the degree to which you avoid the following
    places or situations because of discomfort or anxiety. Rate your
    amount of avoidance when you are with a trusted companion and
    when you are alone. Do this by using the following scale.

>   1 = Never avoid
>   2 = Rarely avoid
>   3 = Avoid about half the time
>   4 = Avoid most of the time
>   5 = Always avoid

>   (You may use numbers halfway between those listed when
>   you think it is appropriate. For example, 3-1/2 or 4-
>   1/2.)

>   Write your score in the blanks for each situation or place under
>   both conditions: When Accompanied and When Alone. Leave blank
>   situations that do not apply to you.

2. After completing the first step, circle the five items with which
    you are most concerned. Of the items listed, these are the five
    situations or places where avoidance/anxiety most affects your
    life in a negative way.

Places	When Accompanied	When Alone
Theatres	_____	_____
Supermarkets	_____	_____
Classrooms	_____	_____
Department Stores	_____	_____
Restaurants	_____	_____
Museums	_____	_____
Elevators	_____	_____

---

*Note: From "The Mobility Inventory for Agoraphobia" by D.
Chambless, G. Caputo, S. Jasin, E. Gracely, and C. Williams, 1985,
Behaviour Research and Therapy, 23, pp. 35-44. Copyright © by the
Pergamon Journals, Ltd. Reprinted by permission.

Places (Continued)	When Accompanied	When Alone
Auditoriums or Stadiums	_____	_____
Garages	_____	_____
High Places	_____	_____
Please tell how high _____		
Enclosed Spaces		
For Example, Tunnels	_____	_____
Open Spaces		
Outside (e.g., fields, wide streets, courtyards)	_____	_____
Inside (e.g., large rooms, lobbies)	_____	_____
Riding In		
Buses	_____	_____
Trains	_____	_____
Subways	_____	_____
Boats	_____	_____
Driving or Riding in Car		
At Any Time	_____	_____
On Expressways	_____	_____
Situations		
Standing in Lines	_____	_____
Crossing Bridges	_____	_____
Parties or Social Gatherings	_____	_____
Walking on the Street	_____	_____
Staying at Home Alone	N.A.	_____

Situations (Continued)	When Accompanied	When Alone
Being Far Away from Home	_____	_____
Other (specify)	_____	_____
_____		

Panic disorder patients average 2.3 (SD = .9) on the Avoidance When Accompanied subscale before treatment and 1.5 (SD = .6) 6 months after treatment. They average 3.4 (SD = 1.0) on the Avoidance Alone subscale before treatment and 2.2 (SD = 1.4) 6 months after treatment.

We define a panic attack as:

1. A high level of anxiety accompanied by
2. strong body reactions (heart palpitations, sweating, muscle tremors, dizziness, nausea) with
3. the temporary loss of the ability to plan, think, or reason and
4. the intense desire to escape or flee the situation. (Note: This is different from high anxiety or fear alone.)

Please indicate the total number of panic attacks you have had in the last 7 days. _____

On the average, how severe or intense have the panic attacks been?

1. Very mild _____
2. Mild _____
3. Moderately severe _____
4. Very severe _____
5. Extremely severe _____

The data on a sample of 232 outpatients with a diagnosis of agoraphobia with panic attacks produced a normal distribution of scores with a mean of 3.19 (SD = 1.00).

SAFETY ZONE

Many people are able to travel alone freely in an area (usually around their home) called their safety zone. Do you have such a zone? _____

If yes, describe:

1. its location:
2. its size (e.g., radius from home):

APPENDIX D: FEAR QUESTIONNAIRE*

Choose a number from the scale below to show how much you would avoid each of the situations listed below because of fear or other unpleasant feelings. Then circle the number you choose opposite each situation.

0	1	2	3	4	5	6	7	8
Would not avoid it		Slightly avoid it		Definitely avoid it		Markedly avoid it		Always avoid it

1. Main phobia you want treated (describe in your own words...................... 0 1 2 3 4 5 6 7 8

2. Injections or minor surgery............ 0 1 2 3 4 5 6 7 8

3. Eating or drinking with other people.... 0 1 2 3 4 5 6 7 8

4. Hospitals............................... 0 1 2 3 4 5 6 7 8

5. Traveling alone by bus or coach......... 0 1 2 3 4 5 6 7 8

6. Walking alone in busy street............ 0 1 2 3 4 5 6 7 8

7. Being watched or stared at.............. 0 1 2 3 4 5 6 7 8

8. Going into crowded shops................ 0 1 2 3 4 5 6 7 8

9. Talking to people in authority.......... 0 1 2 3 4 5 6 7 8

10. Sight of blood.......................... 0 1 2 3 4 5 6 7 8

11. Being criticized........................ 0 1 2 3 4 5 6 7 8

12. Going alone far from home............... 0 1 2 3 4 5 6 7 8

13. Thought of injury or illness............ 0 1 2 3 4 5 6 7 8

14. Speaking or acting before an audience... 0 1 2 3 4 5 6 7 8

15. Large open spaces....................... 0 1 2 3 4 5 6 7 8

*Note: From "Brief Standard Self-Rating for Phobic Patients" by I. M. Marks and A. M. Matthews, 1979, Behaviour Research and Therapy, 17, pp. 263-267. Copyright © 1979 by the Pergamon Journals, Ltd. Reprinted by permission.

16. Going to the dentist..................... 0 1 2 3 4 5 6 7 8

17. Other situations (describe)............. 0 1 2 3 4 5 6 7 8

TOTAL _____

Now choose a number from the scale below to show how much you are troubled by each problem listed, and circle the number.

0	1	2	3	4	5	6	7	8
Hardly at all		Slightly troublesome		Definitely troublesome		Markedly troublesome		Very severely troublesome

18. Feeling miserable or depressed.......... 0 1 2 3 4 5 6 7 8

19. Feeling irritable or angry............. 0 1 2 3 4 5 6 7 8

20. Feeling tense or panicky............... 0 1 2 3 4 5 6 7 8

21. Upsetting thoughts coming into
    your mind.............................. 0 1 2 3 4 5 6 7 8

22. Feeling you or your surroundings are
    strange or unreal...................... 0 1 2 3 4 5 6 7 8

23. Other feelings (describe).............. 0 1 2 3 4 5 6 7 8

TOTAL _____

How would you rate the present state of your phobic symptoms on the scale below?

0	1	2	3	4	5	6	7	8
No phobias present		Slightly disturbing/ not really disabling		Definitely disturbing/ disabling		Markedly disturbing/ disabling		Very severely disturbing/ disabling

Please circle one number between 0 and 8.

APPENDIX E: MAUDSLEY OBSESSIONAL-
COMPULSIVE (MOC) INVENTORY*

		Subscale
1.	I avoid using public telephones because of possible contamination.	2
2.	I frequently get nasty thoughts and have difficulty getting rid of them.	3
3.	I am more concerned than most people about honesty.	4
4.	I am often late because I can't seem to get through everything on time.	2
5.	I don't worry unduly about contamination if I touch an animal.	2
6.	I frequently have to check things (e.g., gas or water taps, doors, etc.) several times.	1
7.	I have a very strict conscience.	4
8.	I find that almost every day I am upset by unpleasant thoughts that come into my mind against my will.	1
9.	I do not worry unduly if I accidentally bump into somebody.	2
10.	I usually have serious doubts about the simple everyday things I do.	4
11.	Neither of my parents was very strict during my childhood.	4
12.	I tend to get behind in my work because I repeat things over and over again.	4
13.	I use only an average amount of soap.	2
14.	Some numbers are extremely unlucky.	1
15.	I do not check letters over and over again before posting them.	1
16.	I do not take a long time to dress in the morning.	3
17.	I am not excessively concerned about cleanliness.	2

*Note: From "Obsessional Compulsive Complaints" by R. Hodgson and S. Rachman, 1977, Behaviour Research and Therapy, 15, pp. 389-395. Copyright © 1977 by the Pergamon Journals, Ltd. Reprinted by permission.

Subscale

18. One of my major problems is that I pay too much attention to detail.   4

19. I can use well-kept toilets without any hesitation.   2

20. My major problem is repeated checking.   1

21. I am not unduly concerned about germs and diseases.   2

22. I do not tend to check things more than once.   1

23. I do not stick to a very strict routine when doing ordinary things.   3

24. My hands do not feel dirty after touching money.   2

25. I do not usually count when doing a routine task.   3

26. I take rather a long time to complete my washing in the morning.   2

27. I do not use a great deal of antiseptics.   2

28. I spend a lot of time every day checking things over and over again.   1

29. Hanging and folding my clothes at night does not take up a lot of time.   3

30. Even when I do something very carefully I often feel that it is not quite right.   3

1 = Checking; 2 = Cleaning; 3 = Slowness; 4 = Doubting

Note: Subscales have unequal number of items.

REFERENCES

American Psychiatric Association. (1980). *Diagnostic and Statistical Manual of Mental Disorders* (3rd ed.). Washington, DC: Author.

American Psychiatric Association. (1987). *Diagnostic and Statistical Manual of Mental Disorders* (3rd ed. rev.). Washington, DC: Author.

Bard, M., & Sangry, D. (1986). *The Crime Victim's Book* (2nd ed.). New York: Brunner/Mazel.

Barlow, D., DiNardo, P., Vermilyea, B., Vermilyea, J., & Blanchard, E. (1986). Co-morbidity and depression among the anxiety disorders: Issues in diagnosis and classification. *The Journal of Nervous and Mental Disease, 174,* 63-72.

Barlow, D., & Waddell, M. (1985). Agoraphobia. In D. Barlow (Ed.), *Clinical Handbook of Psychological Disorders* (pp. 1-68). New York: Guilford.

Barrios, B., & Shigetomi, C. (1979). Coping skills training for the management of anxiety: A critical review. *Behavior Therapy, 10,* 491-522.

Beck, A. T., & Emery, G. (1985). *Anxiety Disorders and Phobias: A Cognitive Perspective.* New York: Basic Books.

Beck, A. T., Ward, C. H., Mendelson, M., Mock, J., & Erbaugh, J. (1961). An inventory for measuring depression. *Archives of General Psychiatry, 4,* 561-571.

Beebe, G. (1975). Follow-up studies of World War II and Korean War prisoners: II. Morbidity, disability, and maladjustments. *American Journal of Epidemiology,* *101,* 400-422.

Bernstein, D., & Borkovec, T. (1974). *Progressive Muscle Relaxation: A Manual for the Helping Professions.* Champaign, IL: Research Press.

Blanchard, E., Gerardi, R., Kolb, L., & Barlow, D. (1986). The utility of the Anxiety Disorders Interview Schedule (ADIS) in the diagnosis of Post-Traumatic Stress Disorder (PTSD) in Vietnam veterans. *Behaviour Research and Therapy, 24,* 577-580.

Cameron, O., Thyer, B., Neese, R., & Curtis, G. (1986). Symptom profiles of patients with DSM-III anxiety disorders. *American Journal of Psychiatry, 143,* 1132-1137.

Chambless, D., Caputo, G., Bright, P., & Gallagher, R. (1984). Assessment of fear of fear in agoraphobia: The Body Sensations Questionnaire and the Agoraphobic Cognitions Questionnaire. *Journal of Consulting and Clinical Psychology, 52,* 1090-1097.

Chambless, D., Caputo, G., Jasin, S., Gracely, E., & Williams, C. (1985). The Mobility Inventory for Agoraphobia. *Behaviour Research and Therapy, 23,* 35-44.

Clarke, J. C., & Wardman, W. (1985). *Agoraphobia: A Clinical and Personal Account.* Sydney, Australia: Pergamon.

DiNardo, P., O'Brien, G., Barlow, D., Waddell, M., & Blanchard, E. (1983). Reliability of DSM-III anxiety disorder categories using a new structured interview. *Archives of General Psychiatry, 40,* 1070-1074.

Eth, S., & Pynoos, R. (1985). *Post-Traumatic Stress Disorder in Children.* Washington, DC: American Psychiatric Association Press.

Fairbanks, J., Keane, T., & Malloy, P. (1983). Some preliminary data on the psychological characteristics of Vietnam veterans with post-traumatic stress disorder. *Journal of Consulting and Clinical Psychology, 51,* 912-919.

Fairbanks, J., & Nicholson, R. (1987). Theoretical and empirical issues in the treatment of post-traumatic stress disorder in Vietnam veterans. *Journal of Clinical Psychology, 43,* 44-55.

Goldstein, S. (1986). Sequential treatment of panic disorder with alprazolam and imipramine. *American Journal of Psychiatry, 143,* 1634.

Hodgson, R. J., & Rachman, S. (1977). Obsessional compulsive complaints. *Behaviour Research and Therapy, 15,* 389-395.

Jenike, M. (1983). Obsessive-compulsive disorder. *Comprehensive Psychiatry, 24,* 99-115.

Jenike, M., Baer, L., & Minichiello, W. (1987). Somatic treatments for obsessive-compulsive disorders. *Comprehensive Psychiatry, 28,* 250-263.

Jerremalm, A., Johansson, L., & Öst, L.-G. (1986a). Cognitive and physiological reactivity and the effects of different behavioral methods in the treatment of social phobia. *Behaviour Research and Therapy, 24,* 171-180.

Jerremalm, A., Johansson, L., & Öst, L.-G. (1986b). Individual response patterns and the effects of different behavioral methods in the treatment of dental phobia. *Behaviour Research and Therapy, 24,* 587-596.

Johnson, S. B. (1985). Situational fears and object phobias. In D. Shaffer, A. Ehrhardt, & L. Greenhill (Eds.), *The Guide to Child Psychiatry* (pp. 169-181). New York: Free Press.

Keane, T., Malloy, P., & Fairbanks, J. (1984). Empirical development of an MMPI subscale for the assessment of combat-related posttraumatic stress disorder. *Journal of Consulting and Clinical Psychology, 52,* 888-991.

Knapp, S., & VandeCreek, L. (1988). A clinician's guide to popular anxiety books. *Private Practice of Psychotherapy, 6,* 17-39.

Koeppen, A. S. (1974). Relaxation training for children. *Elementary School Guidance and Counseling, 9,* 14-21.

Krystal, H. (1968). *Massive Psychic Trauma.* New York: International Universities Press.

Lang, A., & Jakubowski, R. (1976). *Responsible Assertive Behavior: Cognitive Behavioral Procedures for Trainers.* Champaign, IL: Research Press.

Last, C., Francis, G., Hersen, M., Kazdin, A., & Strauss, C. (1987). Separation anxiety and school phobia: A comparison using DSM-III criteria. *American Journal of Psychiatry, 144,* 652-653.

Lazarus, A. (1976). *Multimodal Behavior Therapy.* New York: Springer.

Lehrer, P., & Woolfolk, R. (1984). Are stress reduction techniques interchangeable, or do they have specific effects? A review of the comparative empirical literature. In R. Woolfolk & P. Lehrer (Eds.), *Principles and*

Practice of Stress Management (pp. 404-477). New York: Guilford.

Liebowitz, M., Campeas, R., Levin, A., Sandberg, D., Hollander, E., & Papp, L. (1987). Pharmacotherapy of social phobia. *Psychosomatics, 28,* 305-308.

Liebowitz, M., Gorman, J., Fyer, A., Campeas, R., Levin, A., Davies, S., & Klein, D. (1985). Social phobias: Diagnosis, pathophysiology, and treatment. *Psychopharmacology Bulletin, 21,* 610-614.

Marks, I. (1978). *Living with Fear.* New York: McGraw-Hill.

Marks, I. (1987). *Fears, Phobias, and Rituals.* New York: Oxford University Press.

Marks, I., & Matthews, A. (1979). Brief standard self-rating for phobic patients. *Behaviour Research and Therapy, 17,* 263-267.

McCann, B., Woolfolk, R., & Lehrer, P. (1987). Specificity in response to treatment: A study of interpersonal anxiety. *Behaviour Research and Therapy, 25,* 129-136.

Michelson, L. (1987). Cognitive-behavioral assessment and treatment of agoraphobia. In L. Michelson & L. M. Ascher (Eds.), *Anxiety and Stress Disorders* (pp. 213-279). New York: Guilford.

Michelson, L., & Ascher, L. M. (1984). Paradoxical intention in the treatment of agoraphobia and other anxiety disorders. *Journal of Behavior Therapy and Experimental Psychiatry, 15,* 215-220.

Neuman, F. (1985). *Fighting Fear.* New York: Bantam.

Öst, L.-G. (1985). Coping techniques in the treatment of anxiety disorders: Two controlled case studies. *Behavioral Psychotherapy, 13,* 154-161.

Öst, L.-G., & Hugdahl, K. (1981). Acquisition of phobia and anxiety response patterns in clinical patients. *Behaviour Research and Therapy, 19,* 439-442.

Öst, L.-G., Jerremalm, A., & Johansson, J. (1981). Individual response patterns and the effects of different behavioral methods in the treatment of social phobia. *Behaviour Research and Therapy, 19,* 1-16.

Öst, L.-G., Johansson, J., & Jerremalm, A. (1982). Individual response patterns and the effects of different behavioral methods in the treatment of claustrophobia. *Behaviour Research and Therapy, 20,* 445-460.

Öst, L.-G., & Sterner, U. (1987). Applied tension: A specific behavioral method for treatment of blood phobia. *Behavior Research and Therapy, 25,* 25-29.

Rachman, S. (1974). Primary obsessional slowness. *Behavior Research and Therapy, 12,* 9-18.

Raphael, B. (1986). *When Disaster Strikes.* New York: Basil Books.

Reich, J. (1986). The epidemiology of anxiety. *The Journal of Nervous and Mental Disease, 174,* 129-136.

Sarafino, E. (1986). *The Fears of Childhood.* New York: Human Sciences Press.

Schwartz, G., Davidson, R., & Coleman, D. (1978). Patterning of cognitive and somatic processes in the self-regulation of anxiety: Effects of meditation versus exercise. *Psychosomatic Medicine, 40,* 321-328.

Sheehan, D. (1984). *The Anxiety Disease.* Toronto: Bantam.

Shipley, R., & Boudewyns, P. (1980). Flooding and implosive therapy: Are they harmful? *Behavior Therapy, 11,* 503-508.

Shore, J. (Ed.). *Disaster Stress Studies: New Methods and Findings.* Washington, DC: APA Press.

Somnier, F., & Genefke, I. (1986). Psychotherapy for victims of torture. *British Journal of Psychiatry, 149,* 323-329.

Spielberger, C. D., Gorsuch, R. L., & Lushene, R. (1970). *The State-Trait Anxiety Inventory.* Palo Alto, CA: Consulting Psychologists Press.

Steketee, G., & Foa, E. (1985). Obsessive-compulsive disorder. In D. Barlow (Ed.), *Clinical Handbook of Psychological Disorders* (pp. 69-144). New York: Guilford.

Sweet, A., Giles, T., & Young, R. (1987). Three theoretical perspectives on anxiety: A comparison of theory and outcome. In L. Michelson & L. M. Ascher (Eds.), *Anxiety and Stress Disorders* (pp. 39-61). New York: Guilford.

Thyer, B., Himle, J., & Curtis, G. (1985). Blood-injury illness phobia: A review. *Journal of Clinical Psychology, 41,* 451-459.

Thyer, B., Parrish, R., Curtis, G., Neese, R., & Cameron, O. (1985). Ages of onset of DSM-III anxiety disorders. *Comprehensive Psychiatry, 26,* 113-122.

Titchener, J., & Kapp, F. (1976). Family and character change at Buffalo Creek. *American Journal of Psychiatry, 133,* 295-299.

Turner, S., & Beidel, D. (1985). Empirically derived subtypes of social anxiety. *Behavior Therapy, 16,* 384-392.

Turner, S., Beidel, D., Dancu, C., & Keys, D. (1986). Psychopathology of social phobia and comparison to avoidant personality disorder. *Journal of Abnormal Psychology, 95,* 389-394.

Turner, S., McCann, B., Beidel, D., & Mezzich, J. (1986). DSM-III classification of anxiety disorders: A psychometric study. *Journal of Abnormal Psychology, 95,* 168-172.

Turner, S., Williams, S. L., Beidel, D., & Mezzich, J. (1986). Panic disorder and agoraphobia with panic attacks: Covariation along the dimensions of panic and agoraphobic fear. *Journal of Abnormal Psychology, 95,* 384-388.

Vanderploeg, R. D., Sison, G. F. P., Jr., & Hickling, E. J. (1987). A reevaluation of the use of the MMPI in the assessment of combat-related posttraumatic stress disorder. *Journal of Personality Assessment, 51,* 140-150.

Van Devanter, L., & Morgan, C. (1984). *Home Before Morning.* New York: Warner.

Weekes, C. (1976). *Peace from Nervous Suffering.* New York: Bantam.

Weekes, C. (1984). *More Hope and Help for Your Nerves.* New York: Bantam.

Whalen, S., DiGiuseppe, R., & Wessler, R. (1980). *A Practitioner's Guide to Rational-Emotive Therapy.* New York: Oxford University Press.

Williams, J. (1987). Revised classification for anxiety disorders. *Hospital and Community Psychiatry, 38,* 245-246.

Wolpe, J. (1981). The dichotomy between classical conditioned and cognitively learned anxiety. *Journal of Behavior Therapy and Experimental Psychiatry, 12,* 35-42.

Wolpe, J. (1982). *The Practice of Behavior Therapy* (3rd ed.). New York: Pergamon.

Wolpe, J., & Lang, P. (1969). *Fear Survey Schedule.* San Diego, CA: Educational and Industrial Testing.

Woolfolk, R., & Lehrer, P. (Eds.). (1984). *Principles and Practice of Stress Management.* New York: Guilford.

Zane, M., & Milt, H. (1984). *Your Phobia.* New York: Warner.

OTHER TITLES IN THE PRACTITIONER'S RESOURCE SERIES

Diagnosis and Treatment Selection for Anxiety Disorders is one of three books now available in the Practitioner's Resource Series. The other two titles are:

Pre-Employment Screening for Psychopathology: A Guide to Professional Practice by Rodney L. Lowman.
(PESH) Paperback: $9.95 + 1.00 shipping   1989   88 pp.
ISBN #0-943158-34-6

Tarasoff and Beyond: Legal and Clinical Considerations in the Treatment of Life-Endangering Patients by Leon VandeCreek and Samuel Knapp.
(TABH) Paperback: $9.95 + 1.00 shipping   1989   76 pp.
ISBN #0-943158-31-1

If you would like to order or receive more information on either of these publications, please call (**Toll Free 1-800-443-3364**) or write (Professional Resource Exchange, Inc., P.O. Box 15560-H, Sarasota, FL 34277-1560), and we will be happy to send you our latest newsletter/catalog. When you call or write, please tell us your professional training (e.g., Psychologist, Clinical Social Worker, Marriage and Family Therapist, Mental Health Counselor, School Psychologist, Psychiatrist, etc.) to be assured of receiving all appropriate mailings.

We are dedicated to providing you with applied resources and up-to-date information that you can immediately use in your practice. Our orders are usually shipped within 2 working days and come with a 15 day no-questions-asked money back guarantee.

Thanks for your interest!

Sincerely,

Lawrence G. Ritt, PhD
President